PETER BRUEGEL THE ELDER

ARTIST OF ABUNDANCE

by H. ARTHUR KLEIN & MINA C. KLEIN

Peter Bruegel's paintings, drawings, and engravings record, just as he saw it, the fascinating, turbulent milieu of the sixteenth century—a troubled era when a new merchant class broke free of old feudal patterns and the struggle began to liberate the Low Countries from Spanish rule.

This lavish pictorial biography reveals that the artist—once dismissed as "Peasant" Bruegel—was an independent thinker, a friend to intellectual leaders of the time, and a thoughtful, compassionate observer. Turning from ornate and imitative fashions prevalent in the art circles of his era, he ranged from satire and sharp social comment to fantastic vision, to rural scenes and studies of endu...

The ...
thr...
ian ...
establ...
this ric...
hundred...
tions an...
vide a sun...
abundant ...
Elder...

H. ARTHUR KLEIN and MINA C. KLEIN have long shared enthusiasm for Peter Bruegel the Elder. They have collaborated on several books, and H. Arthur Klein is also the author of *The Graphic Worlds of Peter Bruegel the Elder*. In addition he has written and produced a variety of educational and art films, including *Bruegel's Seven Deadly Sins*, made from the engraving series of the same name. Mr. and Mrs. Klein live in Malibu, California.

Jacket photographs: *front*, detail of *Peasant Dance*, or *Kermess* (courtesy of Kunsthistorisches Museum, Vienna); *back*, detail of *Skaters Before the Gate of Saint George in Antwerp* (courtesy of the Philadelphia Museum of Art).

Peter Bruegel the Elder

ARTIST OF ABUNDANCE

MESSINA

Peter Bruegel the Elder

ARTIST OF ABUNDANCE

*An illustrated portrait of
his life, era, and art
by* H. ARTHUR KLEIN
& MINA C. KLEIN

THE MACMILLAN COMPANY, NEW YORK

The Macmillan Company,
New York
Collier-Macmillan Canada, Ltd
Toronto, Ontario

Library of Congress catalog
card number: 68-20616

Designed by
Herbert M. Rosenthal

Printed in the
United States of America

First Printing

Verse translation on page 102
from *Graphic Worlds of Peter
Bruegel the Elder*, by H. Arthu
Klein, Copyright © 1963 Dove
Publications, Inc., New York.
Reprinted by permission of th
publisher.
Quotations on page 82, from
"Boats in a Fog," and on
page 170, from
"Autumn Evening," both by
Robinson Jeffers, are from
*Roan Stallion, Tamar and
Other Poems*. Copyright 1924,
1925, Boni & Liveright;
copyright renewed 1951, 1953
by Robinson Jeffers. Reprinted
by permission of
Random House, Inc.

frontispiece:
Detail of *Naval Combat in the
Straits of Messina;* engraved
by Frans Huys, 1561
(Los Angeles)

title page:
Bruegel's signature as engraved
and etched by him, detail of
Landscape with Rabbit Hunters
(Boston)

For
Josephine
and Jake Zeitlin
in appreciation,
affection, and friendship

Contents

Acknowledgments

Thanks are offered to a number of individuals whose cooperation and kindness aided in the research, writing, and illustration of this book.

The special indebtedness to Jake and Josephine Zeitlin of Los Angeles is suggested by the dedication.

Valued stimulation came also from a number of Bruegel-lovers resident in or near Brussels: John and Beatrice Barrell; Johan and Oty Reyne-Lebeau; Emmanuel and Suzanne Rycx, occupants of that same "Kasteeltje" at Pede Sainte-Anne where Bruegel himself once worked; Georges Marlier, distinguished art historian and critic; and Bob Claessens, whose vigorous lecture, *Aimer Bruegel* (Brussels, 1963), provided ideas of keen interest.

The Belgian Information Service, through Frans Maes, director, and Joseph Kadijk, deputy director, in New York City, was helpful especially in the photographic area.

Much translating of new material from French was accomplished with the aid of our friends Lauri Provencher and Toni Littlejohn.

Access to research materials at the Los Angeles County Museum of Art was generously given by Ebria Feinblatt, Curator, Prints and Drawings. We were privileged also to use, and now to thank for, the abounding facilities of the library systems of the University of California at Los Angeles and of Los Angeles County. Thanks for the former are extended to Dr. Robert Vosper and his friendly staff; and for the latter to Deborah B. Wilds, regional librarian, and also to Jill McGrew and Tony Dorn, staff of "our" faithful bookmobile.

A score or more of heads and staff members of great galleries and collections in Europe, Britain, and the

United States must go unmentioned here; they have been otherwise informed of our thanks. However, we cannot omit mention of the generous and deeply valued pictorial assistance of the National Gallery of Art, Washington, through the agency of Miss Colles Baxter, Assistant, Graphic Arts; and Dr. E. R. M. Taverne of the Kunsthistorisch Instituut, University of Nijmegen, the Netherlands.

For errors of statement, whether through commission or omission, the authors assume sole responsibility, and will welcome corrective communications from interested readers.

H. Arthur Klein and Mina C. Klein
Malibu, California, 1968

List of Illustrations

Paintings, drawings, and engravings are
by Peter Bruegel the Elder unless otherwise noted.
P = Photographic source when it is not the indicated owner.

Color Plates

Following page 140

The Prospect Before Us

This book is formed from the works and the life of an extraordinary artist: Peter Bruegel the Elder. His brief creative career ended four centuries ago in Brussels. Today his paintings and drawings, and the engravings made from them, are treasured in great museums and collections throughout the world.

Bruegel occupies a remarkable place in art. His name and pictorial ideas were never more important than now. Scholars and critics devote much attention to his works. A vast Bruegel literature has accumulated— articles, monographs, books, even films—and continues to grow.

Yet far more fascinating than the comments of those who study his pictures, are—in the opinion of the authors —the pictures themselves. This fascination may touch you, too, from the reproductions in the following pages and from the enjoyment of still other great pictures that could not be included.

Bruegel's power is not always easy to explain. It seems to arise in spite of, or perhaps *because* of, con- tradictory qualities. To most of us today his pictures appear

both *simple* and *subtle,* in their style;
both *familiar* and *strange,* in their meanings;
both *clear* and *cryptic,* in their symbols.

Always, and emphatically, his works are marked by richness, variety, and abundance. Even, at times, by exuberance. Yet they are almost never gay and certainly never trivial.

The abundance is a matter of content, not of count. The pictures known to be his works are, in fact, not numerous. All together—paintings, drawings, and engravings made from them—the number is less than three hundred. Many a mediocre or minor artist has left far more!

Bruegel is above all an "abundant" artist because of the rich life and imagination he has recorded; because of his broad interests and penetrating curiosity; and because of his urge to preserve rather than disregard the details, tasks, and concerns that made up the daily lives of ordinary men, women, and children of his land and era. His art is inclusive, not exclusive.

Bruegel stands at a crossroad. He sums up many tendencies inherited from the Middle Ages; yet he also leads into the best of the art that followed in later centuries. This book, however, considers Bruegel mostly in relation to his own agitated era.

Very little is *known* of the personal events that made up his life. The few facts that seem certain are included in the life story which follows. Where we have had to suppose or guess, we have said so. This is not a work of fiction. It builds on certainties by means of probabilities or even likely surmises, but it does not seek to masquerade the latter as the former. Bruegel's pictures, however, tell us so much about his world and his thought that his becomes, in fact, an abundant life story.

The situation is not unlike that of Shakespeare, another abundant and versatile creator. The dated facts of his life are scarce; the puzzles and problems are many. Yet, thanks to his wide-ranging mind and his magic of poetry, he puts us in touch with so much of human life that he cannot seem a stranger, even to this era.

Ebria Feinblatt, Curator of Prints and Drawings at the Los Angeles County Art Museum, has called Bruegel not only the "greatest Netherlandish artist of the sixteenth century," but also "the first and most important popular artist in the history of Europe." This is in the original and principal sense of *popular*, pertaining to the common people, for toward the end of his life he allied his art with the situation and struggles of the masses of people around him. Bruegel, during the twentieth century, and especially in the years since the 1940's, has become also a popular artist in the other sense: namely, beloved or approved by large numbers of the people.

This book, then, explores the essential Peter Bruegel the Elder, artist of abundance. It tells in words what can be told with assurance about his wonderfully creative life. Primarily, though, it tells of that life and its times through his pictures, the products of that creativity. His pens and brushes were guided by one of the greatest visual imaginations in all art history. He spoke so eloquently to and for his era that he speaks also to us across the intervening centuries.

I *The Quiet Apprentice at the Print Shop of the Four Winds*

1 Detail of *Village amid Woods*, or *Pagus Nemorosus*, engraving (page 86)

The year was 1548. The city—Antwerp on the Scheldt River, Europe's most dynamic commercial and financial center.

Not far from the busy Bourse, or Stock Exchange, and at the corner of the Rempart Sainte Catherine and La Court Rue Neuve, the sign *In de Vier Winden* (At the Sign of the Four Winds) announced the opening of a new shop for fine prints and other art objects.

Significantly, that art enterprise is remembered today chiefly because of its association with a quiet and dedicated young man named Peter Bruegel. He was certainly the most gifted and original of the ambitious apprentice artists who mingled with its visitors and customers. Four hundred years later he would be ranked as the greatest artist of his century in all the Low Countries, the region now known as Belgium and the Netherlands.

Typically, Bruegel listened more than he talked. But mostly he observed, often sketching and accumulating many pages of pictorial notes for the future.

Jerome Cock, the enterprising proprietor of the Four Winds, had returned in 1548 from a lengthy observation of leading art centers in Italy, in preparation for launching a new art shop in his home city of Antwerp. Always alert for new talent to publish, he was eager to offer his patrons fine prints by artists of the Low Countries as well as imports from Italy, Germany, and other outside sources.

When Master Cock first became acquainted with him, Bruegel was apprenticed to a successful and facile artist-decorator named Peter Coecke van Aelst. Like his fellow apprentices under the rules of the Guild of Saint Luke, Bruegel was not yet allowed to sign, offer, or sell what he drew or painted. He worked as his master directed, and what he produced belonged to that master. Regardless of talent, an apprentice remained dependent on his master for contact with the growing world of art patrons and purchasers. The master in turn was bound to instruct, guide, feed, and house him. Such a term of service might run five or six years, after which the apprentice hoped to become a master in the Guild.

Some time between 1548 and the end of 1550, when Coecke van Aelst died, Peter Bruegel entered the service of Jerome Cock, who had been a master since the year 1546. In Cock he found a mentor who, quite clearly, was able both to appreciate and to encourage his originality. Cock, a passable engraver on copper though not a particularly gifted artist, was nevertheless intelligent, ambitious, and alert. Aged forty when he opened the Four Winds, he had by no means lost his zest for new trends in art—or for trends so old that they would appear novel to his customers. He remained in touch with graphic art production in Italy, in the German principalities of the Holy Roman Empire, and—most especially—he knew what was likely to appeal to the connoisseurs and customers of Antwerp and other centers in the Low Countries. He was adept in guiding them to accept the novel and unusual in art.

As a knowledgeable publisher of prints from copperplate engravings, Master Cock actively provided such guidance. The tireless, inspired pen of Peter Bruegel became one of his most useful and persuasive aids, for Bruegel swiftly developed into an outstanding designer of drawings intended and suited to be engraved on copper, and thus reproduced again and again.

In 1551 Bruegel was finally admitted as a free master in the Antwerp chapter of the Guild, or Brotherhood, of Saint Luke. Now he had the right to choose his subjects, to sign and sell his work, to accept commissions. He even had the right to become a master to future apprentices, and the privilege of acting as agent or merchant for the sale of the works of other masters, as Jerome Cock did at the Four Winds.

Among the more than three hundred masters of the Saint Luke's Guild were artists and artisans who worked in a variety of fields. They included the *Schilders* (painters and graphic artists), so called because their craft had originally been that of designing and decorating the shields and coats of arms of the aristocracy and knights; the *Huiscrivers*, who would today be

2 Detail of Stradanus, *Copperplate Engraving and Printmaking* (top of page 4). At the left a pressman is operating a hand press; the man in the background is grinding ink, and the craftsman on the right is daubing ink onto the engraved plate.

known as interior decorators, though they also designed for house exteriors; the *Glaswerkers*, or creators of decorative glassware; and the *Spegelmakers*, to whom ornate fine mirrors owed their existence. In addition, in this era when the horse was the advanced mode of transportation and indispensable to warfare, the Saint Luke Guild also included the *Zadelaers*, *Gorelmakers*, and *Boomhauers*—respectively, the designers and makers of harnesses, saddles, and saddlebows!

It was common for a master artist of the Saint Luke Guild to work during the same year within more than one of these areas. Thus Bruegel's first master, Coecke van Aelst, had executed many commissions for interior and exterior decorating, for design of fine and costly glassware, and even for design of tapestries and rugs— as well as making prettified paintings and drawings in the Italian style.

It was, moreover, an era of expanding horizons and novel enterprises in art, as well as in geographic exploration and commercial organization. It was well into a period of which Ulrich van Hutten, the German poet and Luther partisan, had said some years before: "The winds of freedom are blowing."

Freedoms different from those Van Hutten had in mind, but nevertheless related to them, seemed to be borne by the breezes from the Scheldt harbor that swept past the sign of the Four Winds print shop.

What did the new freedom in art mean to Bruegel? Into what forms did he cast and develop his enormous talents during his short but effective career as a full-fledged free master? Bruegel's work falls into four groups:

1 DRAWINGS *he made expressly to be converted into copperplate engravings and then printed, often called "designs" for engraving;*

2 FINAL DRAWINGS—*not meant for the engraving process (but sometimes engraved, nevertheless, because of their appeal);*

3 PRIVATE DRAWINGS—*essentially graphic jottings and "notes" intended for his own use in later finished drawings or paintings;*

4 PAINTINGS—*mostly in rich, full color, but several in grisaille, a palette restricted to varying degrees of gray or brown.*

Bruegel made memorable contributions in each of these four art forms, but it was through the first that he began to speak pictorially to his fellow countrymen and also to his contemporaries outside the Low Countries.

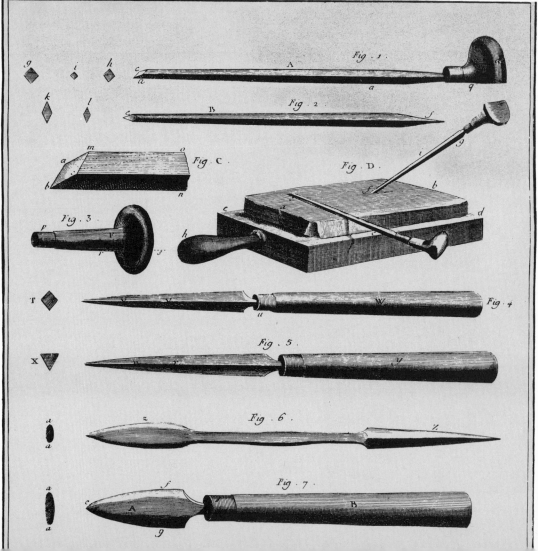

3   *Top Left,* Stradanus,
*Copperplate Engraving and
Printmaking;* engraved by
Philip Galle (Antwerp).
Although more mechanized
today, engraving procedures
are essentially unchanged since
Bruegel's time.

4   *Bottom left,* Engraver's
tools, plate 1 of the *Diderot
Encyclopedia.* Fig. 1 and 2 are
the engraver's burins, and
Fig. C is an enlargement
showing the burin's shape; *g, i,
h, k, l* are all cross sections of
the burin; Fig. D is the sharpen-
ing block, and Fig. 3 is the
burin's removable handle.
Figs. 4 and 5 are scrapers, T
and X their cross sections, and
Figs. 6 and 7 are burnishers,
with cross sections at the left.

5   *Below,* the apprentice drawing (*a*) and the master
engraver with apprentices (*b*),
details of Stradanus, *Copperplate Engraving and Printmaking* (top left)

a

b

Some earlier interpretations of Bruegel's life and
achievement suggest that his whole heart and soul
were absorbed in painting, but that he was forced to
make designs for engravings to earn a living. The real
Bruegel, as the following pages should make clear,
was neither a reluctant draftsman nor a frustrated
painter. He was both a many-sided, powerful graphic
artist *and* a painter of superlative attainments who continued to break new ground until his early death in 1569.

In his own lifetime and for generations afterward
he was far better known and more widely appreciated
as a graphic artist—which is to say, as a designer of
engravings—than as a painter. Many thousands of his
compatriots of the Low Countries—Flemings of the
regions around Antwerp and Brussels as well as
"Dutchmen" or "Hollanders" in the north around
Amsterdam, Rotterdam, and so on—knew him as the
"inventor" of many prints of exceptional power and
impact. These prints were widely purchased, studied,
and discussed.

His paintings, on the other hand, became the private
property of a few aristocrats and men of wealth.
Except for those taken as subjects for engravings after
his death, most of them were not widely known until
much later. Thus it is in the light of the engraving
processes, their possibilities and limitations, that one
must first approach Bruegel.

The techniques of making artistic fine prints from
engraved metal plates were still being developed in
1548 and the years following. In tracing them, one
learns not only something of what Bruegel himself
must have learned as an apprentice in Antwerp to
Coecke and later to Jerome Cock, but also how he began
his career as a free master after 1551.

Two great revolutions in reproduction, or in mass
communication, took place within little more than a
hundred years during the fifteenth and sixteenth centuries. One was the revolution in communication by
words, brought about by the development of printing
from movable type. The other was the revolution in
communication by means of pictures and nonverbal
images, brought about mostly by the development of
metal plate engraving and printing. Both these new kinds
of printing resulted in manifold duplication of carefully
prepared originals. And the cost per copy of the results
was far less than by previous hand methods.

Books were initially printed from movable type less than a century before the opening of the Four Winds in Antwerp. Gutenberg and his associates began such novel work in the 1450's.

During the centuries before, illustrations and even lines of text had often been printed from wood blocks. Such blocks were carefully cut by craftsmen who removed *all but* those areas that were to transfer ink onto paper. Thus printing from wood blocks and from movable type were alike in one thing: both were "relief" printing. The highest surfaces of the printing form made the inked marks on the paper.

Wood block prints might be charming or even powerful, but they suffered from serious limitations. The pronounced grain of wood prevented fine precision of detail and shading, while the comparative softness of wood caused the blocks to wear away too rapidly. "Relief" cutting thus remained crude and clumsy compared with the precision and clarity of lines engraved on metal.

Engraved copperplates were printed in a way opposite to that of wood blocks and raised type. The lines scratched into the metal became, in fact, tiny channels that held ink. The flat top surface of the plate was wiped quite free of all trace of ink, and made no mark. In the press, sheets of damp paper were rolled hard against the metal plate, and ink was transferred from the grooves onto the paper. This is "intaglio" printing.

A single well-engraved copperplate could become parent to dozens, scores, possibly even hundreds of almost identical prints. Even when such a plate began to show wear and the former beautiful "bite" and sharpness of its lines became blurred, there were ways to rework it. Perhaps it could not be restored to its former state, but it might yet be used to turn out another edition or two of salable prints.

Quantity production and identity of product were thus the hallmarks of printing from metal plates. Popular pictures, maps, charts, diagrams, or even ornamentally lettered texts could be duplicated many times and widely distributed. As wealth flowed into a greater number of hands, potential purchasers increased, too. Prints sold through establishments such as Antwerp's Four Winds shop brought returns that sufficed to pay the original artist-designers, the engravers who had transferred the design to metal, the

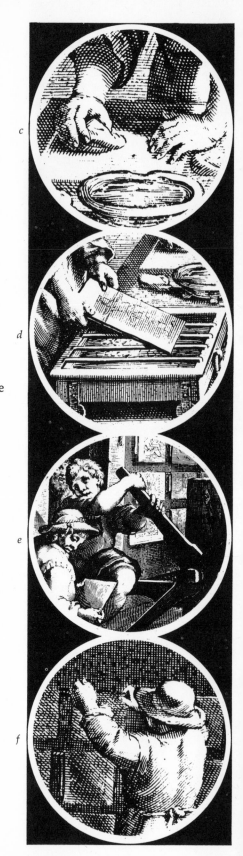

c

d

e

f

6 Further steps in the engraving process: (*c*) wiping excess ink from the engraved plate; (*d*) heating the inked plate so that the ink will become soft and moist and make a clear impression; (*e*) pressman printing; (*f*) hanging up the printed proofs to dry. Details of Stradanus, *Copperplate Engraving and Printmaking* (top of page 4)

papermakers, printers, and apprentices, and still leave handsome profits for the publisher-merchant, such as Master Jerome Cock.

Metal engraving was not new in 1548, nor in 1448, for that matter. During thousands of years ornamental designs, often intricate, had been scratched or punched into such metals as copper, bronze, gold, silver, and tin. Engraving for printing, however, did not date back beyond about 1400 A.D. Suitable printing papers had not previously been available in sufficient quantities, and further, the market for such prints remained quite restricted until about the fifteenth century. Technology had to combine with suitable social and economic conditions in order to make possible a flowering of graphic reproduction methods and the resulting art styles.

Artistic prints from engraved metal were originally made in Italy, Germany, and the Low Countries during the first half of the fifteenth century. In the Low Countries the first such prints are known to have appeared about 1440. From that time until about the opening of Cock's Four Winds in 1548, engraving in that region was influenced largely by examples previously produced in what are now Germany, Austria, Czechoslovakia, Hungary, and Switzerland; and also, somewhat later, by Italian examples.

Jerome Cock himself, during his important sojourn in Rome, 1546–48, had carefully noted the methods of such Italian print enterprises as those of the Barlachi, the Ducceti, and the Lafreri families. Though at first following in their footsteps, Cock's Four Winds soon moved in directions characteristic of the distinctive culture of the Low Countries.

Cock was more than a master in the artists' Guild of Saint Luke. He was also a master of what today is often called "merchandising." Art has need for great innovators and organizers as well as creators of genius, and Cock's place in his era and after is well suggested by Arthur M. Hind in his *History of Engraving and Etching, from the 15th Century to the Year 1914,* published in 1923. This author, formerly Keeper of Prints and Drawings at the British Museum, listed the leading sixteenth century engravers of the Low Countries and described them collectively as "engravers under Italian influence, working largely for publisher-engraver Cock."

II Bruegel's Antwerp: City at the Crossroads of the World

7 Detail of *Skaters Before the Gate of Saint George in Antwerp*, engraving (page 43)

Great movements and innovations in art do not arise
in a vacuum. The social soil, the climate of ideas, and
the economic foundations all must be favorable. This is
illustrated by the circumstances surrounding the great
upsurges that brought the renaissance in art to Florence
and other towns in Italy. It is also shown most strikingly
in the case of Bruegel's city of Antwerp, a swiftly
growing center in the extraordinary and strategically
placed region—the Low Countries.

As Rome was called the city of the seven hills, so
Antwerp had been known as the city of the seven
gates. Beginning in the second or third decade of the
sixteenth century it could claim another and more
significant title: the city of the seven seas. It developed
into the biggest, busiest port and trade center of the
Western world. Antwerp, four hundred years ago, was
the great goods handler of Europe. Hundreds of vessels
arrived and departed daily, bringing and taking cargoes
of merchandise.

But beyond this traffic in necessities and luxuries,
Antwerp became Europe's foremost banking and finance
metropolis. In its busy Exchange and commercial offices
originated enterprises and ventures that operated all
over Europe, and in the New World also.

Even monarchs turned to the money men of Antwerp
to borrow funds for their armies, their campaigns, their
intrigues. Throughout Europe strong, centralized
monarchies were developing. Their rulers made war
with growing frequency, employing large, expensive
armies of mercenaries, equipped with ever more costly
weapons.

The era of Antwerp's ascendancy was about 1520–80,
and its peak coincided with the probable dates of the

life of the artist Peter Bruegel, who is thought to have been born between 1525 and 1530 and known to have died in 1569.

During this period of rapid and accelerating change, Antwerp attained a position unique in its world and, indeed, in history. Never before, never again since, did a single metropolis draw to itself so commanding a share of international commerce, capital, and financial control.

The Low Countries region, thanks to its strategic position and the direction of flow of the great rivers whose sediments had formed its flat soil, had become even during the Middle Ages the prime commercial center of northern Europe. Then came the discoveries and colonial conquests of the Portuguese and Spaniards and the Italian Christopher Columbus, which shifted southern Europe's commercial center as well, from the Mediterranean to the Atlantic. During the middle third of the sixteenth century this meant Antwerp, above all.

8   Virgilius van Bologne and Cornelis Grapheus: Printers' district and waterfront (1565), detail of *Air View of Antwerp* (Antwerp)

Antwerp excelled in more than wharves and warehouses, ships and longshore labor. It was not merely the world's great shipping center, but the center for a new economics that broke free from the traditional safeguards, limitations, and restrictions of the Middle Ages. Like a magnet Antwerp drew the most aggressive capitalists and commercial adventurers from all over Europe, bringing their funds, their bills of exchange, their paper evidences of debts and credits.

They operated from Antwerp as from a great command post, amassing profits, and profits upon profits. In Antwerp as nowhere else they were free of the old barriers enforced by the guilds, the corporate bodies, and the communes during the medieval period.

The transition from medieval methods of production and distribution to the methods of modern times first took place in Antwerp. Modern, militant capitalism was born, or at any rate passed out of its early infancy, there. The new patterns that emerged in Antwerp were followed elsewhere in the Low Countries, and then in much, though not all, of the rest of Europe.

Antwerp's prosperity was outstanding. It flowed from her Bourse and banking houses and warehouses into the rest of the Low Countries. And where money and profits accumulate, the attention of the world follows. No other city was so cosmopolitan. Merchants, financiers, speculators, and downright adventurers had

VRBS

PARS

BECKHOF

FORVM POMARIV

PORTAS IOAN
DARVM

VIA
RVSTATB
E TERREÆ

VIA CAMERARIA

VIA LONGOBARDICA

flocked to Antwerp from all sides: German, Italian, French, Spanish, Portuguese, English, Polish, and others.

Lodovico Guicciardini, an Italian who had long lived there, described sixteenth century Antwerp in his book *A Description of All the Low Countries:*

> *"It is indeed amazing to see such a mass of men of so many different temperaments and kinds. And . . . more wonderful still to find such a variety of languages, differing so much from one another. . . . Without leaving one town you can see, and even imitate exactly, the manner of living and habits of many distant nations."*

No matter where they came from, all were drawn by the prospect of profits. Guicciardini said it was hard to believe how busy Antwerp citizens were in buying and selling, storing and shipping, commodities of all sorts. These included metals from German mines, wines from France, spices from the Orient, grains from agricultural areas, wool and cloth from England.

Still other commodities, essential to the true story of Peter Bruegel's art, were among the exports and imports of this unparalleled metropolis on the Scheldt River: prints, maps, books, pamphlets, decorative objects of gold, silver, and glass. Even paintings and sculptures came and went in the art trade at Antwerp.

The good things of life—including intriguing art, satisfying music, and fine food and drink—were never in short supply for those who could pay. Even the admiring Guicciardini remarked, rather doubtfully, that the love of luxury here was perhaps greater than good sense could defend.

Evidences of this prosperity were the more than three hundred active painters, sculptors, and decorative craftsmen enrolled in the Antwerp chapter of the Guild of Saint Luke. The well-to-do citizens of the Low Countries were proud of their artists. It was the kind of pride that supported the latter's growth and livelihood.

Carel van Mander, himself an artist as well as art historian, wrote at the end of the sixteenth century: "Antwerp, in our Netherlands, seems to have been the mother of artists, as was Florence in Italy in ancient times. Antwerp produced many artists who displayed a great variety of work."

Antwerp's prosperity and that of the Low Countries in general was put to very practical use by the powerful Emperor Charles V, their ruler since 1520. He taxed the region at a higher rate than any of his other European domains. The Low Countries were not only the most densely populated of his territories, they were also the wealthiest, and Charles, whose ambitions were enormous, extracted about 40 per cent of his general revenues from them. And still he called for more.

The Emperor had been born in the Low Countries himself. He knew its languages (Flemish and French) and understood, in general, how not to trespass too far on its traditions or minimum rights. Thanks to an intricate series of royal marriages and dynastic inheritances, Charles V was the most powerful monarch in all Europe. He ruled Spain, Milan, the Kingdom of Naples, and the domains of the Austrian House of Hapsburg. He was also the elected emperor of that assemblage of mainly Germanic states called the Holy Roman Empire —but well said to have been neither holy, Roman, nor imperial in its make-up.

Most important or perhaps unfortunate: Charles "aspired to universal dominion," as pointed out by the great Belgian historian, Henri Pirenne. He intrigued and sometimes fought, though without permanent success, against his great foe, the king of France. He

9 Peasant, *From the Life*, pen and ink drawing, c. 1564–65 (Rotterdam)

Quid modo divitiæ, quid fului vasta metalli
Congeries, nummis arca referta novis,
Wel aen thy Spaerpotten. Tonnen, en Kisten,
Tis al om aelt en ghelt, dit striden en twisten.

Illecebres inter tantas, atq. agmina furum,
Inditium cunctis efferus Oncus erit,
Al jettmen v oic anders, willet niet gheloouen,
Daerom vuere wy den haec die ons noyt en misst,

Preda facit furem, feruens mala cuncta ministrat
Impetus, et spolijs apta rapina feris.
Men soeckt wel altie om ons te verdooven,
Maer men souwer niet krygen, waerder niet te roouen.

intrigued also against the ambitions of Henry VIII, the Tudor king of England. And when he found the Pope in Rome cooperating too closely with the king of France, Charles staged a bloody invasion of Rome itself, and held the Pope for ransom. After this violent episode papal policy was shaped pretty much as Charles desired.

Among the problems that confronted Charles V and the governors who represented him in the Low Countries was unrest among the thousands of people who had been thrown out of their former protected employment by the operations of the new capitalists centered in Antwerp. Town workers, once secure under guild regulation of output and working conditions, began to wander out, jobless, into the countryside where the new men of wealth set up their factories and work-houses. There were villages in the neighborhoods of Hondschoote, Armentières, Ypres, Lille, and elsewhere,

10 The Fight of the Money Bags and the Strong Boxes; engraved by Peter van der Heyden, c. 1558–67 (New York). In this battle of symbolic money-holding monsters Bruegel brilliantly satirizes the ruthless commercial rivalry so evident in Antwerp, the dominant financial and shipping center of northern Europe during his lifetime. The costly wars of ambitious rulers frequent in that era are also suggested. Note the three French words at lower right beneath a fallen warrior (money chest): "Aux Quatre Vents"—the name of the print shop directed by Jerome Cock.

in which a new and basically vulnerable class began to appear in numbers: industrial workers without resources, with no fixed employment, and without the former guild protection on wage rates, hours of work, apprenticeship conditions, and so on. It was a strange reverse migration, *from* the towns into the rural regions.

This great army of destitute and insecure industrial workers provided labor for a new cloth trade, whose product went to the Antwerp market. It helped also to create the new coal and iron industries in the provinces of Hainault, Namur, and Liège. But there were no safeguards for these workers who had nothing else to offer but their labor and no resources to fall back on when they could not sell that.

New, sharper contrasts and conflicts arose: the fabulous wealth and power of relatively few in Antwerp were set off against the hunger and despair of many from the towns and the countryside.

Since ideas then flowed largely in religious channels, social discontent was manifested in demands for reform of the established religious structure: the Roman Catholic Church, ruled from Rome. Dissent had begun in Germany with Martin Luther's protests and final defiance, just about the time Charles was elected Holy Roman Emperor in 1520. Luther's writings, and those of other Protestant reformers such as Huldreich Zwingli and John Calvin of Geneva, filtered into the Low Countries. This flow was halted neither by the strict decrees against Protestant writings nor by the Inquisition set up to wipe out heretical ideas.

The new ideas, in fact, made headway and gained adherents. Literacy was higher in the Low Countries than in most parts of sixteenth century Europe, and even among the peasants an unusual number could and did read. The underground presses published banned Bible translations in Flemish and French. The works of Luther and his advocates, of Calvin and his supporters, and many sharp, critical, or satirical writings and drawings circulated widely, passing from hand to hand till worn out.

It was a time of increasing stress. The tension could be sensed in Antwerp behind the facade of luxury and plenty. Here a new, more ruthless and demanding group had gathered, described by the historian Pirenne as "bold adventurers, great merchants, bankers, and speculators, as keenly devoted to the search for wealth

as was the humanist to the knowledge and wisdom of
antiquity, and as devoid of scruple as a diplomatist
trained in the school of Machiavelli."

Their activity, Pirenne points out, caused a parallel
development between art history and economic history.
These new capitalists were no more like the patricians
of the Middle Ages than the works of Raphael were
like those of Fra Angelico in Italy; or the works of
Frans Floris, the great "Italianizer," were like those
of Jan Van Eyck in the Low Countries.

In fact, these "new men," typical of Antwerp and
what it stood for in the world, were the economic
conquistadors of their eras. As Pirenne asserts, "They
had no ancestors, no family traditions, and their fierce
eagerness to acquire riches manifested itself with that
peculiar intensity and vigor which characterize all new
forces set free at that passionate period." And it was
this period that needed—and found—a genius to record
and interpret some of its most striking and contra-
dictory aspects—Peter Bruegel the Elder.

Major struggles of the period are reflected in this
sensitive artist's work, even though, so far as is known,
he never painted the portrait of a king, a prince, a
duke, a governor, a general, nor any other member of
the ruling class. Nor did he work directly for them,
though his works in later years were eagerly sought
after and treasured by members of the powerful House
of Hapsburg, to which belonged both Charles V and
his son Philip II, the Spanish-reared martinet who was
to become the stern ruler of the Low Countries.

Bruegel was still an apprentice in 1549 when
Charles V, that imperious and ceremony-loving monarch, made an official announcement of utmost importance to his Flemish subjects: accompanied by Philip,
now twenty-two, he would make ceremonial visits to
Brussels, Antwerp, and other centers of the Low
Countries.

Their object was not merely pageantry. Charles's
health was failing. He had ruled nearly thirty years. He
was worn by repeated wars, intrigues, and physical
illnesses. Now he had decided to transfer to Philip
the rule of his vast and scattered domains. In particular
he was concerned that the Low Countries, richest gem
in that strangely assorted multiple crown of his, should
pass to Philip still united, loyal, and yielding the
revenues essential for further warlike undertakings.

In Antwerp on the Scheldt, the "Grand Entry"—as the state visit of Charles and Philip was called—became a momentous occasion. The city leaders were eager to please Charles, whose favor they had long courted for the sake of the special freedoms he allowed their merchants and capitalists, and they also wanted to make a favorable impression on Philip, who would soon become their ruler.

To glorify Antwerp for the great event, Bruegel's first master, Coecke van Aelst, a specialist in approved classical ornamentations and graphic display, was called on to direct hundreds of artists, decorators, craftsmen, and their apprentices. Peter Bruegel was probably one of this small army of the arts.

The results were memorable, or at least they seemed so to the proud Flemings. Coecke felt he had done his city, his sovereigns, and himself great credit, and in 1550 he published at his own expense an illustrated work commemorating the Grand Entry. Its engravings almost certainly were made from designs that Coecke himself had supplied. In a sense it formed his farewell to a world in which he had done well, materially speaking, for Coecke died in that year.

Bruegel and his fellow apprentices probably had plenty to talk about before, during, and after the adventure of the Grand Entry. Despite its pomp and the elaborate assurances of undying loyalty to the hereditary monarchs, father and son, there was a bitter aftertaste. It arose from basic differences between the future ruler, Philip, and his Flemish subjects. And it boded ill for the time when Philip would reign.

The prosperous burghers of Antwerp and other cities in that part of the Low Countries were partial to festivals and festivities, just as Signor Guicciardini had noted. They sought and found occasions to feast, drink, dance, and celebrate. They admired genial hosts, gourmandizers, hearty drinkers, and tellers of tall tales. They were repelled by the sour-faced, the strait-laced, the secretive, and the sternly formal.

Philip, they discovered during this state visit, was all these things. It was all too clear that for the Low Countries he felt neither affection, sympathy, nor even understanding. Around Philip moved a retinue of haughty Spanish courtiers and priests, their stilted manners reflecting and reinforcing his own. He was fluent in neither the Flemish-Dutch nor the French

11 Details of *The Battle Between Carnival and Lent*; oil on wood panel, signed and dated 1559 (page 118)

language, nor did he think in ways that most Low
Countries men could fathom.

Nevertheless, the stubborn and carefully laid
schemes of Charles V were carried out. Half a dozen
years later, in 1555, amid elaborate rites and sentimental
observances, he transferred to Philip the rule of the
Low Countries—all seventeen provinces, united in a
bond that, so Charles declared, was to be indissoluble
for all time to come. (Within barely a dozen years
thereafter, the northern provinces, the area now called
the Netherlands, had begun their successful fight for
independence.)

In 1556 Philip became also king of Spain and monarch of all his father's lands in Italy and the New World,
and the next year he visited his kingdom of the Low
Countries. He appointed, as had become customary, a
regent or governor to represent him there. She was his
half-sister Margaret of Parma, an illegitimate daughter
of Charles V, and Flemish on her mother's side.

Then Philip II left the Low Countries, never to set
foot in them again. He did not, however, leave them
alone; nor did they give him and his advisers in Spain
much cause for comfort during the years that followed.

Thus two great areas of conflict overlapped and
intensified each other in the Low Countries, and especially in the focal regions of the great cities of Antwerp
and Brussels, the latter being the seat of government
and of the Regent's court. One area of conflict involved
the drastically changed patterns of production and
distribution of goods, with the resulting social dis-
turbances. The other involved the domination of the
increasingly unified, proud, and independent-minded
Low Countries by what was all too clearly a foreign
regime—that of Philip II of Spain, distant in miles,
in manner, and in outlook.

These two conflicts combined, and together they
formed an explosive mixture that detonated during the
lifetime of Peter Bruegel the Elder. And only by calling
attention to these great ferments around him is it
possible to make clear just how deeply involved in his
time and place was this artist who graphically recorded
so many of the most memorable situations and attitudes
of that era. Bruegel lived in a most dynamic region of
a most dynamic part of the world—and during a period
of transition and tension whose impact we are better
able to perceive because of his abundant genius.

12 Vredeman de Vries:
Jerome Cock and his wife at
the Four Winds print shop,
from *Scenographiae sive
perspectivae*, published by
Jerome Cock in 1563
(Amsterdam)

III Certainties and Uncertainties About Names, Places, and Dates

13 St. Jerome and the lion, detail of *St. Jerome in the Desert*, engraving (page 85)

Peter Bruegel is the name used here for the subject of
this book about a very human and humane artist. Yet
his name appeared in many other forms during his
own lifetime, as it has since.

The 1551 entry that showed he had been made a
free master of the Antwerp Brotherhood of Saint Luke,
the artists' guild, gives the name as *Peeter Brueghels*.

His first name is elsewhere often spelled *Pieter*, a
fashion still prevalent in the Netherlands.

As for his last name, such varied forms as Bruegels,
Brueghel, Breughel, and two or three others provide
clues to the painter's period and place of residence.
They reflect the easy-going attitudes toward spelling
in the sixteenth and even the seventeenth centuries,
and the dual-language pattern of the Low Countries.

Two great language currents met along an imaginary
line that lay somewhat south of Brussels. North of this
line the prevalent tongue was Flemish-Dutch, a so-called
"Low-German" language; to the south it was
French-Walloon, a Romance language which, like
modern Spanish and Italian, had developed from
modifications of old Latin.

Bruegel grew up speaking the Flemish-Dutch of the
sixteenth century. It was much like the language today
spoken in northern Belgium and throughout the
Netherlands. Yet he and his educated friends were
also fluent in French, the language used in court circles in
Brussels and by many aristocrats and wealthy families.

Latin remained the international language of
scholarship and learning. Also in the southern Low
Countries, or what is today Belgium, the often
unwelcome Spanish language reflected the presence of
the Spanish troops, first of Charles V, then of Philip II.

Bruegel's earliest pictures were signed *Brueghel*. The *h* was not sounded, and the *ue* was pronounced somewhat like the *ay* in *bray*, and even more like the *eu* in such French words as *feu* or *jeu*. This is a vowel sound not duplicated in English pronunciation today.

About 1559, the artist discarded the *h* and began to sign his pictures BRUEGEL, in characteristic and handsome capital letters [14]. His greatest paintings and drawings, completed during the final decade of his life, were thus signed. So we follow here the free and final choice of the master himself.

That does not end the story. When Bruegel died in the autumn of 1559, he left his widow with two young sons: Peter the Younger was four or five years old; Jan, only one year old. Both grew up to become professional painters, and both commonly spelled their name *Breughel*. This not only restored the silent *h*, but substituted the French *eu* combination for the Flemish *ue*. It is, therefore, no typographical error to say that Peter Breughel the Younger and Jan Breughel were sons of Peter Bruegel the Elder.

To compound the possible confusion, art dealers and collectors often added the master's name to drawings he had not himself signed. At times they used such spellings as *Brugell* or even *Brögel*.

The name Bruegel, or some near variation, was not unknown nor even exceptional in the Low Countries during the sixteenth century. Records have been found of several citizens thus named. They were townsmen, not peasants.

Often it has been assumed that Bruegel's name indicates the village or district where he was born, in the region of the Low Countries called the Campine. In fact, Carel van Mander, in his *Schilderboek* (Book about the Painters) published more than a third of a century after Bruegel's death, flatly stated that he was "born not far from Breda in a village called Brueghel, a name that he took for himself and his descendants."

That statement does not harmonize, however, with the entry in the rolls of the Antwerp artists' guild, *Peeter Brueghels*. That final *s* implied something like "the Brueghels' Peter," or even "Peter, of the Brueghel family," rather than "Peter, from the Brueghel place."

There are, however, several towns in Bruegel's homeland which bear that same name, and three of them claim to be his birthplace. All lie east of Antwerp.

14 *Wilderness of Rocks with Gorge and Castle*; pen and ink drawing, dated 1561 (Rotterdam)

15 Travelers, detail of *Wilderness of Rocks with Gorge and Castle*

One is in the province of North Brabant, part of the present Netherlands. The other two lie some thirty miles to the south in the Belgian province of Limburg, near a town called Brée. These are the twin villages known as Kleine-Brögel (Little Bruegel) and Groote-Brögel (Big Bruegel).

The Netherlands village is located a few miles north of the well-known industrial city of Eindhoven. It is sometimes called Brueghel-Son, for it lies within the parish of "Son." This village contains a rather recent monument honoring the great artist, who, the memorial declares, was born there.

The two Belgian villages make the same claim. The tradition in the region is that the painter was born in a big old farmhouse in the Groote-Brögel parish, called Ooievarrsnest, which means "stork's nest." This old house lies between Brée and a town called Peer. Brée, several centuries ago, was known as Breda or Brida. Hence those who regard this as Bruegel's birthplace quote Van Mander's statement that the master was born "not far from Breda in a village called Brueghel."

This could, of course, apply also to Brueghel-Son in the Netherlands, for that, too, is near a Breda—the present-day Breda, about thirty miles from Eindhoven.

The truth of this tangle is that one cannot now positively prove just where Bruegel was born, or even where he spent the first dozen or more years of his short but influential life.

But though Bruegel's birthplace cannot be pinpointed, he was assuredly a Fleming from "the Campine" and the Brabantine region. There is today no political unit or province called the Campine, but Belgium's central province of Brabant surrounds the capital city of Brussels, and just north of the border, in the Netherlands, lies the province of North Brabant.

It is sometimes said that Bruegel was born in Brussels itself, but though that city is his burial place, there is no shred of evidence that he was born there, nor, for that matter, in Antwerp, where he was trained and began his amazing career in art.

Bruegel's birth is believed to have occurred within a range of six years: 1525–30. The first exact date that we can assign in his life, however, is that 1551 entry in the master-rolls of the Guild of Saint Luke of Antwerp. The rank of master was achieved only after years of

16 Detail of *Sloth*; engraved
by Peter van der Heyden, 1558
(page 98)

apprenticeship in art. Few prominent painters became
masters before the age of twenty, but it is unlikely that
an artist so talented would be obliged to wait until he
was past twenty-six or twenty-seven.

A few scholars, impressed by the abundance and
maturity of Bruegel's achievements between 1551 and
his death in 1569, believe he may have been older
than twenty-six when he became a free master. Surviving
works show that by 1552 he was already drawing with
marvelous authority and effectiveness, and some fine
paintings have been attributed to him which may have
been done as early as 1552, or within the several years
following.

Bruegel's birth *may* have been as early as 1524
or even 1523. But that is sheer guesswork. And no
matter when he was born, the wonder remains: how
could an artist develop so far and in so many different
directions within a mere seventeen or eighteen years
after his career as a free master began?

IV *An Education in Art*

17 Detail of *Children's Games*; oil on wood panel, signed and dated 1560 (plate II)

Bruegel's education as an artist is more important than the precise time or place of his birth. The ground here is firmer, too, for Carel van Mander, in his brief biography of Bruegel, declares that he "learned his craft from Pieter Kock van Aelst" (a name now commonly spelled Coecke or even Coeck).

Bruegel must have shown promise to be accepted as apprentice to Coecke, who, at about that time, was the dean, or deacon—that is, the honorary head—of the Antwerp Guild of Saint Luke, and also was a court painter by appointment to the Emperor Charles V.

Coecke's art, though now it may appear rather shallow and artificial, was esteemed by influential people in his own time. He was an artistic success, a man of the world, a versatile craftsman, accomplished in glass decoration, sculpture, tapestry design, interior decoration, and ornamental display.

Coecke's works today hang in a number of museums. They are competent, Italianate, decorative, and usually embellished with many accurately drawn architectural details. An example is Coecke's *Adoration of the Kings* (or Magi) [18]. Through the archways to the right of the mother and child, figures can be seen at several distances. Everything recedes in harmony with the laws of correct perspective, all the way back to the remote hills, which are amply supplied with small details.

Except for this miniaturistic treatment of the distances, there is little to link this static and prettified piece to Bruegel's subtle, powerful, and deeply moving masterworks. We can make a comparison, for Bruegel later made two different paintings on the subject of the *Adoration of the Kings*. Though unlike each other, each differs drastically from Coecke's.

The better of these two paintings [19] hangs in
London's famed National Gallery, bearing Bruegel's
signature and the date 1564. Like most of his paintings,
it was executed in oil-based pigments on wooden
paneling—not on canvas or linen fabric. All the
paintings reproduced in this book are such "oil on
wood" creations unless otherwise noted.

Mother and child sit outside a crude shelter. Before
them kneel two of the kings, offering frankincense and
myrrh. The third, at right, dark-skinned and with
light garments, bears jeweled offerings. Joseph is the
white-bearded, stout, grandfatherly looking figure
behind Mary. A young man whispers in his ear. (Is
he perhaps warning of the massacre that King Herod
has ordered against infants in the Bethlehem area?)

A Roman soldier holding a sharp pike looks on,
wide-eyed; a crossbowman stands at his side. Eight or
nine other onlookers stand around, intently watching
the strange events. They are varied but common Low
Countries types.

Every person, including Mary and Joseph, is plausible.
They are human beings—ordinary, not extraordinary,
homely and solid rather than glamorous or supernatural.
They are people such as Bruegel could and must have
seen and sketched time and again during his keen-eyed
observations in the busy streets of Antwerp or Brussels
or even to the north in Amsterdam. They are earthy,
even coarse, individuals, but genuine rather than
idealized; they have not ceased to breathe and sweat.

The face farthest right is that of a bespectacled
peasant or artisan. Spectacles, of course, were unknown
in the days of Jesus, but Bruegel—even more than
Shakespeare, with whom he has many affinities—was
beautifully anachronistic. Sometimes, it almost seems,
deliberately so.

King or carpenter, magistrate or stablehand, soldier
or saint—all are offered with equal simplicity, direct-
ness, and candor. Nothing is ornamented or elaborated.
Nothing is distorted into an appearance of luxury or
aristocratic sophistication. A great gap lies between
these believable humans of Bruegel and the decorative
compositions fashioned by Master Coecke van Aelst!

From such evidence one may conclude that though
Bruegel may have worked busy years as an apprentice
under Coecke, he took little or nothing from that
master's manner in art—at least nothing discernible

18 Peter Coecke van Aelst,
Adoration of the Kings; cente
panel of triptych, oil on wood,
c. 1525 (Princeton, New Jerse)

19 Peter Bruegel the Elder,
Adoration of the Kings; oil or
wood panel, signed and dated
1564 (London)

today. This suggests an exceptional self-direction and independence of mind on Bruegel's part, and these were, indeed, qualities in evidence more than once during his later career as a creative free master.

Perhaps a more lasting influence on this gifted apprentice was Coecke's second wife, Marie (or Maeyken) Bessemers Verhulst, a skillful and accomplished painter of miniatures. It is possible that during Peter Bruegel's period of apprenticeship in the Coecke household and studio she began to instruct him in techniques of miniature painting, using water colors and other pigments, for among Bruegel's later masterpieces we find striking numbers of tiny, precise details, especially in the far distances. Though he did not scale his complete paintings in miniature sizes, he used methods familiar to the miniaturists to enrich his scenes and to express his vision of reality.

The upper right-hand segment of his *Children's Games* [17], for example, a teeming painting dating from 1560, portrays a long straight street in a Low Countries town, stretching away a mile or more in perfect perspective. All along this street groups of children are playing their various games, no two of them alike. (The full painting is reproduced in plate II.) Even at the most distant visible point this street is punctuated by a precisely drawn detail: a tiny building whose tower measures little more than half an inch on the painting itself. Small size does not mean vagueness or lack of accuracy.

Many a Bruegel landscape can be appreciated in full detail only with the aid of a good magnifying glass.

Another example is offered by the famous painting of rural life and labor in midwinter, often called *Hunters in the Snow* [20], one of Bruegel's marvelous cycle of "Seasons" landscapes (see also plate III).

Snow blankets the land. On a frozen pond, men, women, and children are skating. About two dozen can be counted, their darker bodies contrasted with the greenish ice. Though so small, their actions are easily identifiable. Beyond them lie church, village, street, stream, houses, trees, banks, hills—stretching into the farthest distance, ever smaller, but nevertheless distinct and accurate.

The Harvesters is another masterpiece of the "Seasons" cycle (plate IV). The detail reproduced [21] is part of the view downward and into the distance,

20 Detail of *The Hunters in
the Snow, January* or *February;*
oil on wood panel, signed and
dated 1565 (Vienna)

looking along inhabited land that gently descends
toward a large lake.

The road running from left to right leads around
a fishing pond. At the extreme right lies a village green
with a dozen or more small human figures, standing,
walking, or running. On the painting itself each figure
is scarcely more than half an inch high. Yet each
appears to be a distinct individual.

Such skill in painting meaningful details on a small
scale does not by itself make a great painter, or even

a great miniaturist or illuminator. However, it was part of Bruegel's special power as a painter.

To some today, miniature painting appears as a kind of freak or game. In Bruegel's era this was by no means the case. Miniaturizing was an admired and well-patronized specialty in sixteenth century art, in Italy as well as in the Low Countries. Royalty, the nobility, and the wealthy sought out fine miniaturists and commissioned them either to make tiny portraits (of themselves or family members) or perhaps to provide intriguing and brilliant illuminations for cherished books, such as missals and breviaries. Some of these illuminations became famous in their own right for their high imagination, their gemlike color, and their elegant though tiny compositions.

Whether or not Marie Bessemers Coecke was Bruegel's guide and instructor in the art of miniature painting, she played a multiple role in his later life. For as Coecke's second wife she became the mother of a "junior" Marie, or Maeyken, who later became Peter Bruegel's wife and the mother of his two sons. Thus Marie Bessemers Verhulst Coecke, the competent miniaturist, became Bruegel's mother-in-law, the grandmother of his two sons, and certainly the teacher of one of them in the miniaturizing arts.

Bruegel is not the only talented apprentice who later married the daughter of his former master. In the case of the marriage of Marie Coecke and Peter Bruegel, however, there is a detail that is told, in miniature fashion, in one of the intriguing anecdotes reported by Van Mander in just two sentences: "Bruegel learned his craft from Pieter Coecke van Aelst, whose daughter he afterward married. Often when [Bruegel] lived

21 Detail of *The Harvesters*, or *The Corn Harvest*, probably *August*; oil on wood panel, signed and dated 1565 (New York)

with Aelst he carried her in his arms when she was little."

Some art scholars have suspected this is a pretty fiction made up by Van Mander to illuminate his Bruegel story. They cannot doubt the fact of that marriage, for the register of the Brussels church of Notre Dame de la Chapelle, for summer 1563, showed an entry of the marriage there performed uniting *Peeter Brugel* and *Maryken Cocks*. But did the apprentice "Peeter Brugel" carry in his arms the infant or tiny "Maryken Cocks" who fifteen or sixteen years later became his wife?

If we sift the probable dates, we find that it *could* have happened. Coecke married Marie Bessemers Verhulst somewhere in the period 1534–36. Marie was most likely born between four and eight years after the marriage, between 1538 and 1544. Thus, when she was married in Brussels in 1563, she was between nineteen and twenty-five, probably closer to the former than the latter figure.

Now "Peeter Brugel" himself at the time of this wedding must have been between thirty-three and forty years old. This would have made him older than his bride by at least eight years, and at most twenty-one years. If Van Mander was right in saying that this groom once had carried in his arms the little girl who became his bride, then this difference in ages can be narrowed somewhat: Bruegel would have had to be at least thirteen years older than "Maryken," and he could hardly have been more than twenty-one years older.

If Bruegel became apprenticed to Master Coecke about the year 1540—which is one possibility, unproved —then "Maryken" could already have been a toddler, or still an infant, or she may even have been born only after the gifted apprentice became part of the Coecke household.

It is certain that Bruegel's marriage took place after he was already an accomplished artist and had been a master for a dozen years; that he married the youngest daughter of the man who had been his first master; and that the pair became parents of two painters, and through them, the progenitors of an impressive number of other artists.

These certainties suffice to make the marriage of Peeter and Maryken an event of some significance in the history of the finest Flemish art.

v A New Artist Amidst Engravers

22 Hunters, detail of *Landscape with Rabbit Hunters*, engraving (page 37)

When Peter Bruegel at last became a free master in 1551, this welcome change in status may not have greatly altered the kind of work he was already doing for Jerome Cock of the Four Winds print enterprise. Yet it probably improved the terms on which that work was done. A free master, as Bruegel now was, could work on his own account, sign and date his pieces, contract with patrons, accept commissions, and retain the agreed payments. He might even go on to take apprentices of his own.

By 1551 Bruegel must have been abundantly familiar with the methods and possibilities of engraving on copperplates, and also of etching, which added to the "scratch" method of engraving the additional, controlled bite of acid, eating into those small trenches in the metal. Both Coecke, his first master, and Cock, his later master, had made many a drawing intended for engraving; and the latter was himself a practicing engraver when the need arose.

During the last two years of the 1540's and the first years of the 1550's the Four Winds shop published a number of prints showing Roman ruins, and also Alpine and mountain landscapes.

Roman and Greek ruins and art objects meant much to the art lovers of Antwerp and the Low Countries, just as Roman and Greek literature meant a great deal to the enlightened of that century. The Renaissance in Italy had largely taken the form, at first, of a rediscovery and extension of art surviving from the classical ages: statues, mosaics, and frescoes, as well as works of literature and philosophy.

The expansion of world horizons in the mid-sixteenth century also stimulated the taste for exotic landscapes

which contrasted boldly with the flat and often
monotonous levels of the Low Countries. The most
dramatic and even melodramatic landscapes available
to a European were those of the Alpine regions. And
beyond the Alps lies Italy.

It was not strange that a talented co-worker of
engravers, as soon as he became a master and could
manage it, would plan a journey to that great center of
accepted art styles—Italy. This is what Bruegel did.
Jerome Cock himself may have suggested or even
financed the trip, for he had visited Italy just three or
four years before.

If Cock gave or loaned Bruegel the money for that
journey, it was a sound investment for him—and for the
art future of the Western world. This pilgrimage
enormously stimulated and enriched Bruegel's work
for the rest of his creative life, though he never became
what his first master Coecke had been, a "Romanist"
or "Italianizer" in his art.

The links between Bruegel and Cock of the Four
Winds were long-lasting and fruitful. They endured a
score of years, until Bruegel's final illness and death.
They had begun two or three years before Bruegel left
Antwerp for Italy; they resumed as soon as he returned;
and they continued even after Bruegel later moved to
Brussels.

It is safe to assume that Bruegel had decided to
design originals for engraving even before his departure
for Italy, and that he thought about this during that
important journey.

Bruegel's independence is striking. Just as he did
not echo the art of Master Coecke, so he did not come
back to Antwerp an imitator of the current fashions in
Rome or Venice. Yet he devoted a large part of his
imagination and attention to an art medium—that of
prints from engravings—in which his original designs
had to pass through the eyes, minds, and hands of
other men—the engravers—on their way to a growing
public.

Bruegel himself was a magnificent engraver and
etcher, as is shown by prints from the one metal plate
he is known to have worked, *Landscape with Rabbit
Hunters*, dated 1556 [23]. The delicate, lacy treatment
of tree leaves and shrubbery indicates what Bruegel
intended in his designs but could seldom secure from the
engravers.

23 *Landscape with Rabbit Hunters.* The only engraving known to have been executed by Peter Bruegel the Elder, dated 1566 (Boston). Both the engraver's burin and the acid solution of the etcher were employed.

An engraver seeking to realize a design made by another artist (or even one of his own) is somewhat like a translator who tries to put a fine piece of writing into another language. Translation has been called "the art of the best possible failure," and the saying can also be applied, with much truth, to engraving. Giorgio Vasari, the Italian art historian and painter, declared in his *Lives of the Most Eminent Painters, Sculptors, and Architects*, written about 1567: "However excellent the engraver, he rarely gives full effect to the manner of him who first conceived the work."

On the whole Bruegel fared better than many another designer of originals that were engraved by other hands. From the first he seems to have drawn so that engravers could follow his designs with relatively little loss or awkwardness. It can be said of Bruegel's best designs, many of which survive, that they are halfway to engravings already. He used the brown inks,

which he mixed himself, and the quill pens, which he
shaped and sharpened himself, almost as if he were
working with engravers' burins on paper.

Especially skillful and subtle was his use of lines
for shading, his handling of foliage, clothes, and other
textures. Competent engravers must have been grateful
to work on the designs of an artist who met them
thus on their own ground, helping rather than hindering
their exacting labors.

Even before he set out for Italy, Bruegel undoubtedly
had clear ideas about the major possibilities of the
engraving process, and how he hoped to serve and be
served by it. Many competent artist-engravers were
active in Antwerp at the time of his departure in 1552.
More were working later. Bruegel must have known
their work, their strengths and weaknesses, in scratching
the challenging blank plates of copper.

One of the Low Countries engravers most often
identified with Bruegel originals was Peter van der
Heyden (Peter of the Meadows), who sometimes signed
the initials P-A-M-E; they stood for Petrus a Merica,
the Greek equivalent of his name. He was born in
Antwerp in 1530, and by 1557 began engraving many
of Bruegel's most powerful original drawings. This
combination of Bruegel–Van der Heyden gave the world
some of the most memorable prints of the entire
sixteenth century.

Even more subtle and resourceful in his engraving
techniques was Philip Galle, born at Haarlem in 1537.
It was he who was to convert into plates of rare sensitivity
and delicacy of gradation some of Bruegel's later original drawings and grisaille paintings.

Bruegel's designs did not always fare so well as at
the hands of Galle and Van der Heyden. Yet among
the surviving prints that are sometimes miscalled
"engravings by Bruegel," the general level is relatively
good. Some even merit the name of masterpieces of
their kind. The devotee of original drawings, with pen
and ink, crayon, or chalk, may feel that engravings
never quite convey the essentials of a great artist's work
in line, but one must approach and evaluate prints
from engravings on the basis of what they are rather
than what they are not. They are not, cannot be, original
drawings. Theirs is a different kind of draftsmanship.
And in the mid-sixteenth century many of the technical
advances of graphics—mezzotint, aquatint, lithography,

*24 The Artist and the
Connoisseur;* pen and ink
drawing, c. 1565–68 (Vienna)
In this haunting drawing
Bruegel recorded a significant
confrontation between a
creative artist (probably
himself) and a smug, wealthy
patron (see text on pages
147–49). Some art historians
believe this is not only a
self-portrait during the final
years of his life, but that it
shows the tormenting effects
of an advanced case of
arthritis.

and photo processes of various kinds—were unknown or even unimaginable.

That Bruegel and the engraving processes got on so well together was due to his intelligence, his imagination, his persistence, and his superb mastery of the effects created by his pens and inks.

VI *His Own,*
His Native Land

25   Detail of *Skaters Before the Gate of Saint George in Antwerp*, engraving (page 43)

Considering its quality and variety, the surviving body of work by Bruegel is truly impressive for so brief a creative life. And what the world retains today is by no means all he drew and painted, for at least a third of his total output has been lost, and perhaps even more than half!

There are about fifty Bruegel paintings, almost all in oil colors rather than tempera, executed mostly on wooden panels rather than canvas. Three of these are in monochrome (grisaille), the rest in colors of enthralling richness and brightness.

There are also some 155 Bruegel drawings, almost all done with pen in various shades of brown ink. A large number of them are designs for engravings. Another important group of his drawings are the "private" sketches made from life and intended to serve as reference material for later finished drawings and paintings. Finally there are about eighty different print subjects made from engravings based on his originals.

Thus fewer than three hundred different pictures can be regarded with assurance as the work either of Bruegel himself or of an engraver following his designs. No date that Bruegel himself placed on any of these works is earlier than 1552, with the single puzzling exception of a drawing dated 1547. Apprentices, however gifted, were not allowed to sign or sell their works themselves. And Bruegel remained, at least technically, in apprentice status until 1551.

Though examples of his youthful or pre-master work are missing, fairly confident assumptions can be made as to the sights and situations that attracted his special interest in this fruitful period. Bruegel's later works include several scenes in and around Antwerp,

showing sights that must have fascinated him while
an apprentice. Antwerp was oriented toward its harbor,
its waters, its seas, and the distant lands that bordered
them, and water in all its aspects constantly preoccupied
Bruegel. Again and again he pictured with devotion
and imagination seas, streams, rivers, estuaries, straits,
canals, and harbors, and all the human gear and labor
associated with them.

One of his finest seascapes is *Marine Landscape
with a View of Antwerp in the Background* [26],
undated but completed probably late in the 1550's or
early in the 1560's. Traces of the black chalk in which
he first sketched it still remain. He completed it with
pen, using several shades of the brown ink that he
mixed himself.

The emphasis here is overwhelmingly on the wind-
whipped sea, which fills more than three-fourths of the
drawing from bottom to top. Antwerp appears only
as a silhouette of towers along the horizon at upper left.
The fierce wind, driving from left to right, stirs the
waves in ragged yet regular march and whips foam
from the wave crests.

A large three-masted vessel and five smaller sailboats
are running before this strong wind or tacking across
it. Another vessel rides under "bare sticks" against
the far horizon, just right of the Antwerp skyline. Heavy
storm clouds hang in the sky at upper right, but
through a cloud-rift breaks a beam of light, illuminating
a church tower on the far horizon.

Everywhere is stress, agitation, and the force of the
storm. Amidst the surging waves appears the strangely
oval shape of an island almost engulfed by the waters.
From its bleak surface rise ominous shapes: a rectangular
gallows frame and a crazily leaning pole surmounted
by a wheel. These dismal devices, used to torture
and execute condemned prisoners, were all too well
known in the Low Countries, and emphasize the sense
of menace in the picture. And the ships themselves are
driving from the sunshine toward the storm.

Bruegel pioneered in painting scenes of snow, ice,
and the landscapes of wintertime, especially as reflected
in the changing patterns of human labor and recreation.
Skaters Before the Gate of Saint George in Antwerp
[27], an engraving by Frans Huys from a Bruegel drawing
dated 1558, shows a scene he must have watched many

26 Marine Landscape with a View of Antwerp in the Background; pen and ink drawing c. 1559–65 (London)

27 Skaters Before the Gate of Saint George in Antwerp; engraved by Frans Huys, after a drawing dated 1558 (Philadelphia)

a time while still an apprentice.

Skating is carried on here with determination, even grimly. More than one beginner staggers or falls, unable to remain upright on the sharp, upcurved skates with their triple bindings. Humans abound, as in so many of Bruegel's most typical pictures. It is possible to identify more than 140 people of varied ages and conditions, from foreground to far horizon.

At lower left (above the name of publisher Cock), a gentleman is drawn along in comfort by the cloak of a skateless servant. Peasants or poor town laborers are fastening on skates at right foreground. On the bridge, a Belgian "covered wagon" has paused while its occupants look down on the sport. There is plenty of action. A man has fallen somewhat left of center. Just left of the curving bridge and of the solid gate itself another has crashed through the ice and is being aided by helping hands.

Still another man holds his woman partner about the waist while he demonstrates how easy and pleasant skating can be. On the bank at right stand excited onlookers. A woman with basket on arm shouts as she points to a fallen skater. Behind her are two cloaked observers, so muffled that they seem to have an especially sinister and chilling look. Could they perhaps be spies or informers for the Inquisition?

In the upper background, to the right of the leafless tree, a game of sixteenth century ice hockey is under way. On the other side of that tree, skaters are performing team drills or follow-the-leader in formation. The leader is the flag-bearing skater.

Garments are as varied as the humans who wear them. A strange-looking trio stand in the foreground, somewhat left of center, their backs toward us. The man in the middle wears a large domed hat. The women on either side are clad in characteristic Flemish cloaks with attached visors, like large eyeshades. A dandy with feathered hat is seen at left center.

Rich and faithful architectural details show the Gate of Saint George in all its dignity. Three towers loom up against the winter sky. At least two belong to churches.

The abundance of individuals, individualities, and activities is part of the essential Bruegel. Typical, too, are many faces turned away or hidden from us, and the almost globular form of the youngster poling along on a small sled at right foreground.

28 *Spring*; pen and ink drawing, dated 1565 (Vienna)

From his apprentice days onward, Bruegel loved the recurring rhythms of the seasons. He was country born, and even in Antwerp, a metropolis of its day, the open countryside lay just outside the city walls.

As apprentice to Coecke van Aelst, a sought-after decorator of the homes of the great and wealthy, Bruegel surely often saw work under way on great estates in the Flemish countryside.

Spring [28], dated 1565 and signed with Bruegel's characteristic printing at lower-right corner, is a masterly drawing. The Flemish words he has placed at the bottom mean: "Spring: March. April. May." They appear also in the engraving by Van der Heyden, published by Jerome Cock in 1570, a year after Bruegel's death.

This is the formal garden of an aristocrat. A dozen or more servants are preparing symmetrical beds of flowers and shrubs. The lady of the manor stands (left center), her shade hat in her right hand, pointing with her left to show the respectful servant beside her just where he is to plant the seed. Next to her a young

girl, possibly her daughter, looks down at a playful
puppy. She and he do not have to work.

Pleasure is also the purpose of a party of aristocrats in
the distance across the stream or canal at upper right.
The richly dressed gallants and their ladies lounge on the
grass or eat and drink at a two-level pleasure bower.
They sing, listen to music, and embrace.

In the more remote distance behind, rise the round
tower and steep roofs of an impressive castle, surrounded
by its typical Flemish moat. A church steeple and
traces of a village are suggested nearby. And in the sky,
not less than a score of birds fly in sweepingly curved
formation.

The workers here are laboring hard. Two are twining
vines into a curved archway. Under a thatched shed
with sloping roof, the spring shearing of sheep goes on.
Two women work with shears, another carries a great
basket full of the fleece. A man grasps the hind legs
of a reluctant ewe, yet to be shorn.

The powerful, rounded, almost sculptured forms of
the workers' bodies are impressive, as are the spherical
shapes of faces and heads, and—once again—many
faces turned away or hidden under hats.

29 Sheep-shearing (above)
and the ladies of the manor
(right), details of *Spring*,
drawing (page 45)

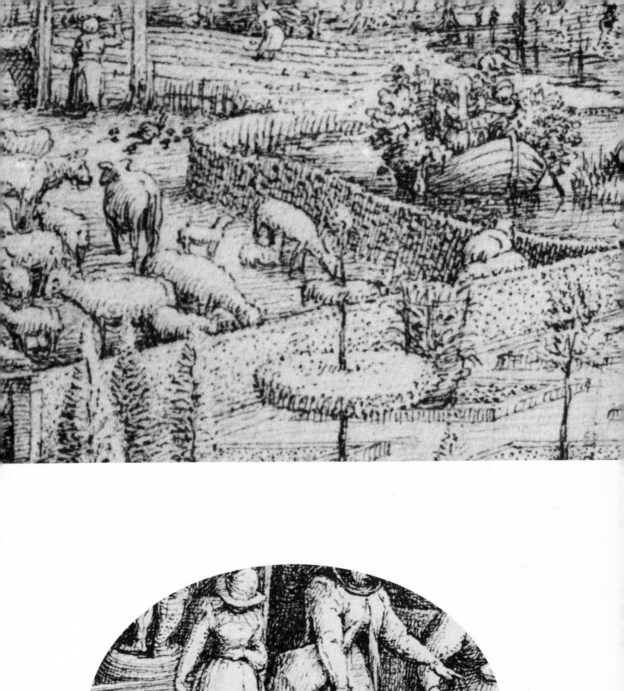

Bruegel knew well the sights, sounds, odors, and labors of summertime also. One of his most admired portrayals is *Summer* [30], dated 1568. This drawing was engraved in 1570, after Bruegel's death. Comparison of the drawing-design and the print [31] reveals that one is a reversal or mirror-image of the other.

Here Bruegel by a bold device produced a striking feeling of solidity, space, and depth: the extended foot of the powerful drinker, and also the handle and blade of his scythe project right out of the picture, past the frame line on the bottom!

An elegant Latin quotation offers a moral to fit this sweltering labor under a blasting sun:

> *"July, August, and also June constitute Summer . . . Summer, the image of youth. . . . Torrid Summer brings to the fields fertile crops."*

These powerful leaning, bending, crouching figures are the men and women who must each year plow, plant, cultivate, harvest, thresh, and store the grains that will be ground into the coarse breads they eat.

This massive and monumental design invites comparison with one of the most famous paintings in Bruegel's "Seasons" cycle: *The Harvesters* (plate IV).

The *Summer* engraving has abundant balance, symmetry, rhythm. The drastic foreshortening of the legs of the thirsty worker at right, the statuesque stance of the scythe swinger at left, the receding levels and layers of labor in the background—all testify to a mastery far beyond Bruegel's apprentice abilities. Yet even for so mature a triumph, the foundations reach back to those days of beginning and learning. Bruegel's lofty

30 Summer; pen and ink drawing, dated 1568 (Hamburg)

Iulius, Augustus, nec non et Iunius Aestas · AESTAS Adolescentiq imago · Frugiferas aruis fert Aestas torrida meßeis ·

31 *Summer*; engraving,
c. 1569 (Washington)

art grew from early roots sunk into the lives of real people on the land and in the towns of Brabant and the Campine.

Again, *Summer* shows Bruegel characteristics: the hiding of many of the faces; the round, almost ball-like contour of the one face shown full (the grain-gleaner, just right of the center line); the careful placing of working humans at many levels, all the way back to the farthest and most miniaturized distances; the ample numbers of houses and human gathering places; and in particular the familiar Flemish church at left rear.

The two massive figures in the foreground have been compared with some of Michelangelo's painted figures that seem almost like statues. Though Bruegel remained free from most Italianate influences, *Summer* shows that he could infuse his composition with harmony, emphasis, and drama comparable to that of the Italian Renaissance masters.

VII From Flemish Lowlands to Mountain Peaks —the Great Journey Begins

32 Artist and companion, detail of *Alpine Landscape with Artist Sketching*; pen and ink drawing (page 53)

Bruegel left Antwerp and journeyed south in 1552. Such a pilgrimage was not unique or even unusual in that era. Among the three hundred registered free masters of the Antwerp Guild of Saint Luke, it is likely that each year at least ten or a dozen must have visited Italy for professional artistic purposes. As Paris once attracted young painters from all over the world, so Italy drew them from northern Europe in Bruegel's time.

The year 1552 became memorable in Bruegel's homeland for several reasons not connected with the fine arts. Two great floods scourged the Low Countries, and a new, more menacing Inquisition was established there. Emperor Charles V empowered Frans van der Hulst, a layman lawyer, to prosecute all heretics as he saw fit. Previously the Inquisition had been headed by churchmen, with established judicial procedures and rules which gave some protection to the accused. Now this "emergency" Inquisitor and his aides were to be allowed to proceed pretty much as they wished. It substituted for a rule of law the wills or whims of ambitious men, eager to win the ruler's favor.

The result was an unfavorable reaction among the citizens of the Low Countries. More of them now felt the cause of accused heretics had become their own, for these arbitrary decrees violated the constitutional or chartered rights of all, not just those of a few zealous Lutherans or Calvinists.

Bruegel traveled southward through France. He doubtless went on horseback or perhaps at times on muleback. A typical day's journey would hardly have exceeded thirty miles. Along the way he paused again and again to feast his eyes on new views and to note them in his sketchbooks.

His baggage must have included sets of chalks, crayons, water colors, drawing papers, and perhaps a portable easel. Safely tucked away were his letters of introduction to artists and men of influence in Italy.

His route took him past important towns in France, among them Lyon, still a famous city. There he sketched a *View of Lyon* and completed it in water colors. It later became a prized possession of Giulio Clovio, leading Italian miniaturist, with whom Bruegel was friendly in Italy. That picture, like so many others whose names alone survive, is unfortunately lost today.

Bruegel's exact route from Lyon into Italy is not possible to reconstruct with total certainty. He may have turned east and then northeast again, following the valley of the Rhone River until he came to Geneva, at the southwestern tip of the lake of the same name in Switzerland. Then he may have continued across Switzerland and entered Italy through a mountain pass from the Swiss canton of Ticino in the lovely Italian-Swiss region.

Convincing evidence, in the form of his drawings and of engravings made from them, indicates that he was in each of these regions before his final return to Antwerp. Yet it is not certain whether this took place on his way *to* Italy or on his way *back*. The plausible choice is that he entered Italy from France, and that his travels in Switzerland took place on the return journey.

It was a memorable meeting in any case, of an artist of immense sensitivity to nature, with natural scenes of enduring drama, even of melodrama. As Carel van Mander vividly declared: "On his journey he painted many pictures from life, so that it came to be said of him that during his visit to the Alps he had gulped down all the mountains and cliffs; and then after coming home again had spat them out upon his canvases and [wood] panels."

Other Low Countries artists returned from Italy as more or less fluent painters in the Italian style. Bruegel, however, brought back, in his notebooks and memory, bold peaks, deeply plunging valleys, far vistas, and rushing streams. He studied a new kind of nature rather than new fashions in painting!

In one drawing called *Alpine Landscape with Artist Sketching* [33], completed in 1555–56 after his return to the Low Countries, Bruegel presents a pictorial echo

33 *Alpine Landscape with Artist Sketching*; pen and ink drawing, c. 1555–56 (London)

of his own manner of work while setting down on paper for future use "all the mountains and cliffs."

As Bruegel often must have done, the small figure of the artist here sits in front of a large boulder, in the foreground just right of center. He is busy sketching a varied landscape: stream, slopes, rocky outcrops, and peaks. Behind him, staring intently over his shoulder, stands a fellow traveler or perhaps a passing native of the region. Quite possibly the artist would prefer not to be so closely watched! A similar situation is found, under indoor conditions, in perhaps the most famous and enigmatic of all Bruegel's drawings, *The Artist and the Connoisseur*, widely believed to contain a self portrait (see pages 39 and 147–49).

The outdoor artist is probably working rapidly with black chalk to set down the main outlines. He may also add written notes to guide him later as to color, light or shade, and textures. Bruegel constantly used

34 *Mountain Landscape with Cloister in the Italian Style;* pen and ink drawing with water colors, dated 1552 (Berlin)

such notes in his scores of life sketches made later in the streets and byways of his Flemish homeland.

By the end of 1552 Bruegel had not only entered Italy but probably traveled all the way down its boot-shaped peninsula. He very likely went beyond the boot itself and crossed the Strait of Messina to the nearby island of Sicily. And in the next year, 1553, he made an extended stay in Rome, the center of "Romanist" art fashions, and the eminent Eternal City of the Western world.

An unusual and fine drawing is *Mountain Landscape with Cloister in the Italian Style* [34]. It was signed and dated 1552, his first travel year. This is one of the two Bruegel works dated so early. It is also the only surviving example of Bruegel's own use of water colors. He drew the lines with pen and brown inks, then added subdued water colors in the appropriate areas.

The nearer hills are touched with green, the more distant with blue-green. Bruegel, in many of his works, magically showed the effect of atmospheric haze in the distance by means of blue and blue-gray tones.

The walls of the nearer wing of the cloister building are tinted brown. The roof is blue-gray, suggesting slate. The roof of the other wing of the building, at right angles to the first, is in a rosy color, indicating red tiles.

The point of view is rather high. This too was typical of a great many Bruegel landscapes, both drawings and paintings, made during and following his Alpine-Italian travels. On that journey he was lifted up, figuratively and actually. He retained always something of this sense of elevation and far-seeing.

At the right, three human figures are roughly suggested rather than carefully drawn. Yet each is individualized. Farthest right, a figure leans against a tree, holding a straight staff, like a resting pilgrim or perhaps a shepherd. The center figure seems to lift a scythe. At left a figure leads a laden horse or mule and has perhaps paused to unload. This man wears a hat with ample brim to protect himself against the burning Italian sun, just as Bruegel undoubtedly did while traveling there.

The preliminary sketch for this picture may have been begun on the spot, not long after Bruegel first began to travel in Italy itself. Expert opinion holds, however, that the drawing was completed in the studio, especially as regards the trees shown in the foreground.

35 Detail of *Mountain Landscape wtih Cloister in the Italian Style*

VIII Sights of Ships and the Sea in Italy

36 Town and rigging, detail of *Man of War Sailing to the Left, with a Town in Background*; engraving (page 6?

Traveling through the historic peninsula of Italy, Bruegel was drawn once more to the world of water—streams, sea, harbors, ships, and sailors.

His intriguing and ornamental painting of *The Harbor at Naples* [37] was probably completed about five to ten years after he first could have seen Naples itself in 1552. It lacks both date and signature, and is painted on wood in colors mixed in oils, rather than in the egg yolks used as the binder in the "tempera" process.

Some experts have doubted that this is a genuine Bruegel, but the weight of scholarly opinion attributes it to him.

This painting is not a photographic record. Liberties were taken here with the actual shape of structures in the Naples harbor of 1552. The jetty or breakwater is shown curving in a smooth sweep in the upper half of the painting, whereas it was actually built in straight lines with angles. Nevertheless, recognizable Neapolitan landmarks are evident: the Castell dell' Ovo (Egg Castle) and the squat tower of Saint Vincent, an island fortress built to defend the harbor. Farther right stands the Castell Nuovo, and on the hill summit just left of center, the Castell Sant' Elmo.

The wind blows freshly toward the right. It molds the lines of waves in the foreground and billows the sails of the proud and stately ships. About ten major vessels, with triple masts and lofty sterns, are scattered about the harbor, as well as dozens of smaller ones.

Drama and conflict are present, also. Two vessels in the foreground, just right of center, exchange cannon shots. Just below the geometrical center of the picture, a ship burns. Such intermingling of marine artillery, flames, and fighting appears also in other pictures stemming

37 The Harbor at Naples, or View of Naples; oil on wood panel, c. 1558 (Rome)

from Bruegel's memorable Italian tour.

Color is boldly but subtly used. The sea is a bronzed green, the sky a radiant golden yellow. The wind has swept an area clear in the sky and piled the clouds toward the right.

This significant marine painting is mentioned several times in old records. In the early 1600's it was in the collection of the Granvelle family, Besançon, France. By 1640, however, it had returned to Antwerp, where it was part of the private collection of the great Peter Paul Rubens, painter-diplomat and a close co-worker of Bruegel's younger son, Jan.

This Naples painting is one of several by Bruegel that show great sailing vessels under way, in combat, or seeking safety in anchorage. Last and most powerful among his marine pictures is the intense painting *Storm at Sea* (plate VIII).

Bruegel appears to have become increasingly engrossed in ships and marine subjects as he traveled south, until, at the very toe of the Italian boot, he came to the coastal town of Reggio di Calabria, on the narrow Strait of Messina, across from Messina, Sicily.

His visit there in 1552 probably took place during a Turkish naval raid that set fire to part of Reggio. The drawing called *Vista of Reggio* [38] shows a great blaze within the walled town, from which billows of smoke stream toward upper left. The raiding ships may have attacked with incendiary shot and flaming pitch—a forerunner of the unspeakable napalm of our twentieth century.

38 Vista of Reggio; pen and ink drawing with wash, c. 1559 (Rotterdam)

In foreground, almost at center, two human figures are silhouetted. The man at right with upraised arms seems to be describing for his companion the attack that caused this blaze. Across the stream on a projecting bank stand two other men, gazing at the burning town.

Though undated, this drawing probably was made in 1559 or a little later. Bruegel drew with pen and dark brown ink on paper with a faintly reddish tinge. Later some other artist added washes of brown and gray and made some other changes at left and in the background hills. These changes, however, do not destroy the power and value of this memorable work.

Closely linked in subject, site, and other ties is *Naval Combat in the Straits of Messina* [39], largest and most imposing of all engravings made from Bruegel's designs. It appeared in 1561, eight or nine years after

Bruegel visited these historic straits and studied the warships there. His original drawing has been lost.

Franz Huys engraved and Jerome Cock published this print, nearly 14 by 17 inches in size. It is so large that it had to be printed from two separate copper plates. The boundary between them is indicated by the "crease" down the center.

The word REZO stands in the sky above the mountains in the distance at left. It indicates that the harbor below is Reggio on the Italian mainland. The word MESSINA appears above that crowded Sicilian port on the other side of the strait. And behind it, looming up with an ominous column of smoke, stands Mount Etna, the formidable volcano which actually lies more than forty-nine miles distant from Messina itself.

In this ship-studded seascape we are looking almost due south from a point on the Italian coast somewhere north of Reggio. Note how, in this engraving as in the previous drawing, streams of smoke rise from Reggio. They show that buildings there had been set afire in the fighting.

Three great naval vessels are fighting at close

39   Naval Combat in the Straits of Messina; engraved by Frans Huys, 1561 (Los Angeles)

quarters in the left foreground. Around them are seven
of the smaller single-masted vessels called galleys. Their
sails are now furled and they are pushed along by
banks of long oars. A typical galley shows clearly at
right foreground. From its side fourteen triple sets of
oars extend, or forty-two in all. Scarcely visible are
the sweating oarsmen within, and their taskmasters and
timekeepers.

Like a symbolic signature of Bruegel, groups of birds
fly high in the sky. The nearest group of two stretch
their long necks, much like the storks the artist so often
showed in the skies of his own Low Countries.

What is this naval struggle, so vast and complex,
in the very throat of the Messina Strait? It is in reality
a sort of composite of numerous battles for marine
supremacy that took place in these seas between the
Turks, who were determined to make the Mediterranean
their "private lake," if possible, and their foes from
Christian Europe, including the forces of Venice, of the
Emperor Charles V, and perhaps also of the Papal States
ruled from Rome.

The galleys streaming out from Messina at right
are probably those of the Turks, while those clustered
around Reggio at left belong to their European foes.

Just about ten years after this print was published,
a historic naval battle was indeed fought not far from
these straits. It was the Battle of Lepanto, October 7,
1571, which shattered Turkish naval power in the
Mediterranean. The hero of Lepanto was Don John of
Austria, who commanded a large, oddly assorted fleet of
vessels supplied by Venice, the Papal States, and Spain.
It numbered more than 300 craft, at least 200 of which
were galleys, each bearing both oarsmen for motive
power and soldiers, or "marines," for boarding actions.
When this fleet assembled at Messina it included about
80,000 men, of whom 50,000 tugged at the great oars!
Thus Bruegel, though his imagination enriched this
picture, surely did not exceed the bounds of possibility.

Bruegel added new observations to his knowledge of
merchant vessels and men of war as he traveled along
the Italian coasts of the Tyrrhenian Sea, as that part of
the Mediterranean is called. In his search for exciting
visual experiences he neglected neither the land nor the
water.

Thanks to his ability to seek out and absorb, he was

able years later to provide his publisher, Cock, with designs for a series of superb engravings which were like glorified portraits of great sailing vessels—great for that era, though tiny alongside an ocean liner or aircraft carrier of our own day. This series has never been surpassed for its feeling of pride, dignity, and eye-filling display of such imposing vessels.

Bruegel's original designs for the series must have been completed by 1563–64. Their engraver was Franz Huys. One of those richest in detail is called *Man of War Sailing to the Left, with a Town in Background* [40].

Here all the sails are furled, but for the large lower sail on the forward mast. A dozen sailors work aloft, from bowsprit to the last, least mast at rear. Each mast carries a small observer's platform, or crow's nest. Rigging details are clearly shown. About a dozen cannon project from the side and two point backward from the stern.

The town beyond the vessel is heavily fortified. It

40   *Man of War Sailing to the Left, with a Town in Background*; engraved by Frans Huys, c. 1562–64 (New York)

41 *Man of War Seen Half from the Left*; engraved by Frans Huys, c. 1562–64 (Washington)

has two protective towers of a type used along the coasts of both the Low Countries and Italy. The heavy stone-walled fortifications extend to the very edges of the water.

In the sky, great clouds pile high. Again, Bruegel's devotion is shown by nine or ten birds in flight.

Another engraving displays a *Man of War Seen Half from the Left* [41]. Nine guns project from its lofty stern structure. They form only part of its armament, however. This imposing vessel carries artillery even on the crow's nest of its main mast, where four small guns point downward.

Seven or eight sailors are here at work or on watch. Each has the rounded, ball-like head and spherical torso that Bruegel so often drew. Clothing and the heavily muscled bodies beneath seem to blend into a single monolithic mass of superimposed globes.

Ahead of the man of war, almost as if flying from it, sails a galley. This is probably a passenger vessel, to judge by the rather elaborate awning that shades its

stern deck. Its oars are raised out of the water. The
wind appears sufficient to propel the vessel without the
aid of human muscle-power.

In Bruegel's ship engravings one sees clearly the
tall, boxlike structures perched on the sterns of these
curved, clumsy hulls. Think of sailing through rough
seas on vessels so prone to pitch, toss, roll, and wallow!
One must admire the sailors of that time, for somehow
they managed to voyage far and wide.

Despite their proud banners and decorations, these
were really small vessels. Those shown in these
engravings probably did not exceed 100 to 130 tons'
displacement, even when fully loaded. A modern ocean
liner would be about 250 or more times as large, and
a giant aircraft carrier, well over 300 times as big!
In fact, it could easily carry a "boat" of 130 tons'
displacement as a tender or auxiliary. Nor was this size
unusual for the time. Philip II's "Invincible Armada"
was reputed to be a concentration of big men of war
when it sailed against England in 1588; yet some 150 of
its vessels averaged less than 390 tons each. And the
fleet that Queen Elizabeth threw together to oppose the
Armada averaged less than 130 tons per vessel.

Even some of the longest voyages of that age of
exploration were made in vessels of similarly small size.
Magellan commanded five vessels, none exceeding
130 tons' displacement. Vasco da Gama's three vessels
that rounded the Cape of Good Hope were each
smaller still.

Men of war bearing down before the wind toward
the right are not the only water-borne objects of interest
in the elaborate engraving called *Three Men of War in
a Tempest, Sailing Right, with Arion* [42]. Three
strange sea creatures swim at lower right. On one of
them sits a naked youth holding a harp, the hero of the
classic myth that Bruegel wove into this rich nautical
design. He is Arion, mythical master musician, almost
on a par with the legendary Orpheus. And the three
strange sea beasts are dolphins, here shown in the
very act of rescuing him.

This picture may be linked with Bruegel's journey to
Messina and across its strait to the island of Sicily.
The legend tells how Arion, after his playing had won
him a prize at a contest in Sicily, shipped on a vessel
to take him to Corinth, his home. The sailors turned

42   *Three Men of War in a Tempest, Sailing Right, with Arion*; engraved by Frans Huys, c. 1562–64 (Washington)

pirate, however, seized his treasure, and started to throw him overboard. He begged them first to let him play for a last time on his lyre.

That lovely sound attracted friendly dolphins. When Arion was finally thrown into the sea, they bore him up and carried him safely to shore. As drawn here by Bruegel and engraved by Franz Huys, the dolphin farthest right seems to be singing a solo to Arion's accompaniment.

The vessel at right appears to have just fired a shot from a cannon slightly above the water line. Bruegel seldom neglected an opportunity to show men of war in action! Nor did he neglect the symbolic sky patrols; two sea birds fly amidst the tempest, in center middle ground.

Another engraving from the great "Ships" series shows a cosmic catastrophe taking place in the sky. A different kind of winged creature has sought to fly

43 *Man of War Sailing to the Right, with the Fall of Icarus;* engraved by Frans Huys, c. 1562–64 (Washington)

here, in this work known as *Man of War Sailing to the Right, with the Fall of Icarus* [43].

According to legend, Daedalus was a great inventor and craftsman. He built the Labyrinth for the King of Crete, but in return the king imprisoned not only Daedalus but his son and helper, Icarus. Daedalus then devised wings with which he and his son escaped and flew over the sea to freedom.

But Icarus, intoxicated with the sensation of flying, ignored his father's warning and soared too near the sun. The wax that held his wings together melted, and he plunged to death in the sea, as shown here in upper right. Daedalus continued flying—alone.

A detail of poignant reality is the feathers that have melted or molted off the unfortunate Icarus and float slowly down below him.

While this human flyer approaches his death, dozens of birds soar at the left, above the rocky land whose cliffs fall sheer into the sea. Should not the sea birds seem smaller at such a distance? An interesting observation has been contributed by John Barrell of Brussels, who writes, "Bruegel's birds appear to be inordinately large, but this proves what a great observer he was. As we were trained to realize in the army, small objects in the sky do look outsize."

The man of war dominating the picture, below Icarus, reveals vivid details of sixteenth century naval construction. From the rear of its lofty forecastle five guns project backward. The gunners who aimed these had to be careful not to strike any part of their own vessel!

To protect sailors against missiles from elsewhere, overlapping shields are fastened to the top of the tall poop deck. On each of the two tall masts is a basketlike crow's nest to which round, shieldlike plates are fastened. Sets of sharp pointed sticks project backward from each of these. They resemble spears stored ready to rain down on enemy vessels during close fighting.

A sailor climbs the rigging of the foremast, on his way from the lower crow's nest to the upper. It appears barely large enough to provide a place for his feet.

This vessel carries eight separate sails. Six are spread, and two smaller ones, on the large mast, are furled. The two mainsails are actually double sheets of canvas, laced together for greater ease in handling. The engraving shows the grommets, or lace-holes, like rivets that join them.

The royal banner, flown from both mastheads, bears the emblem of the double eagle. Does this suggest that the vessel is in the service of the royal House of Hapsburg?

In the lower right-hand corner, like a finishing touch of fantasy and exuberance, a large dolphin whips through the water in a sharp curve, its great mouth agape.

The myth of the rash human flier who fell to his death in the sea attracted Bruegel more than once. It furnished the theme for one of his most haunting earlier paintings, known as *Landscape with the Fall of Icarus*, executed in oil paints on a wood panel, probably about 1555 [44]. No other mythological subject appears in any surviving Bruegel painting.

There are, in fact, two painted versions, closely similar but not identical. Art scholars hold various views as to whether either or both were painted by

Bruegel's own hand, or whether, possibly, one or both are close copies of a lost original that Bruegel did paint. There is no doubt, though, that they both reproduce Bruegel's design, color, and conception, if not his actual brush strokes.

The painting shown here does not picture Daedalus, though Icarus is just being swallowed up by the sea; only his legs are visible above the waves at the lower right. The sun is low over the horizon. Is it dawn? If so, how could there have been heat enough to melt Icarus' wings? Or is this sunset? In that case, Icarus must have been falling for hours, since his wings were melted by the blazing heat of midday!

Enormous irony radiates from this tender and somehow mysterious painting. The "hero" Icarus is barely seen. One must search to discover even the last trace of him. Meanwhile, the work of the world goes on, utterly unaware of his catastrophe. Bruegel has closely followed the scene as described by the Roman writer Ovid. A plowman at left plods along behind his horse. His crude wooden plow forms curved furrows in the soil. A shepherd leans on his staff, gazing at the sky while his sheep peacefully graze. At lower right, a fisherman casts his line into the water. None of them appears to be aware of Icarus' fall.

Still another haunting reminder of human mortality and the indifference of the world appears in the bushes near the left center of the painting; it is a round white object lying beyond the plowed furrows [45]. Only close inspection reveals it as the neglected corpse of an old man!

This painted *Fall of Icarus* reveals much of what makes Bruegel both unusual and enduring as an artist. He stresses the unimportance of a single human life amidst the vastness of nature and the daily realities of toil in the struggle to survive. Even a figure as bold and tragic as Icarus vanishes with barely a ripple on the surface of the sea or in the lives of nearby men and animals.

This silent mockery of ego and ambition is so pointed that one feels the picture must present a parable or proverb. Some have suggested the proverb, "Pride goeth before a fall," since Icarus' rashness brought about his downfall and destruction. There is an old Flemish saying, however, that fits even better: "No plow stands still just because a man dies."

44 *Landscape with the Fall of Icarus;* oil on wood panel, originally painted c. 1555, later transferred to canvas (Brussels)

45 Head of a corpse, detail of *Landscape with the Fall of Icarus*

IX Rome— and the Tower of Babel

46   Arches, detail of *The Tower of Babel*, engraving (page 74)

In 1553 Bruegel spent an important period in Rome. The Eternal City was then the seat of government of the Papal States as well as the headquarters of the Roman Catholic Church hierarchy that was urgently seeking new ways to resist and even to reverse the Protestant Reformation.

At that time Bruegel was probably between twenty-five and thirty years old. What sort of human being was he? The evidence, direct and indirect, indicates that he was quiet and reserved, yet warm and cordial in his human contacts—a thoughtful and unusually silent man, but not gloomy or depressing—a person well able to form and retain friendships with those he felt drawn to.

A half-century later Carel van Mander summarized what people who had known Bruegel had told him of the great artist's personality: "a quiet and a competent man, not much given to talk, but good fun in company." More than that, a practical joker, one who "liked to frighten people, oftentimes his own art pupils, with the various kinds of spooky sounds and tricks that he played."

The scanty clues from Bruegel's Roman visit confirm this picture of the subdued but likable man, attractive to people of intelligence, culture, and humane attitudes. A man, in short, utterly unlike the mistaken image of the "Peasant Bruegel," as he has often but erroneously been called during the centuries after his death. He was anything but an ignorant, ill-mannered boor who by some queer quirk happened to possess genius. The real Bruegel was indeed remembered long and with enduring affection by the cultured and intellectual friends who knew him best as a man and as an artist.

A companion of Bruegel on at least part of his travels
in and around Rome was another Flemish painter,
Marten de Vos, born about 1531–32, hence probably
about the same age as Bruegel himself, though by
no means possessing a similar artistic style. De Vos's
paintings hang today in many European art galleries. He
is said to have worked as an aide in landscape painting
to the great Tintoretto (1518–94) of Venice. It has
been suggested that Marten may have collaborated to
some extent on one of Bruegel's early paintings,
*Landscape with Jesus Appearing to His Apostles at the
Lake of Tiberias* (1553). If so, they must have worked on
it together in Rome.

Bruegel seems also to have become friendly with
a distinguished Italian geographer-scientist, Scipio
Fabius, when both were in Rome or possibly Bologna.
About eight years later Fabius, writing the Netherlands
geographer and cartographer Ortelius, asked after
the welfare of his most dear friend, "Petrus Bruochl,"
as he spelled it. Four years later, in 1565, Fabius again
asked Ortelius to give his regards to Bruegel. These
letters also mention Marten de Vos in a manner that
suggests Fabius must have come to know both
painters when they were visiting Italy together.

Here, as later in his native Low Countries, Bruegel's
personal contacts were with eminent men, in the
forefront of the intellectual and scientific advances of
their era—geographers, humanists, writers, publishers,
printers.

Another close associate of Bruegel in Rome was the
Italian painter and miniaturist, Giorgio Giulio Clovio
(1498–1578), sometimes called Macedone or Macedo
because of supposed Macedonian ancestry. Clovio
was at his artistic best in historical subjects and portraits.
He drew with skill and fine precision, in such detail
as if he were inviting examination under magnifying
glass or microscope. In fact, he stands as one of Italy's
outstanding miniaturists of the age. Vasari referred
to him as "a small and new Michelangelo," and Vasari
was one of Michelangelo's greatest admirers. No wonder
Bruegel appears to have been attracted to Clovio's
work, and he to Bruegel's.

Clovio's high valuation of pictures that Bruegel
completed while still in Italy is revealed by the former's
last will and testament and by the records of the estate
left after his death. They list among his possessions

three Bruegels: (1) the water color of Lyon, France, mentioned earlier; (2) a water color of a tree; and (3) a miniature Tower of Babel, painted on ivory.

The miniature is especially interesting because both Bruegel and Clovio had painted within its tiny confines. This collaboration expressed their joint enthusiasm for the art of miniature. Unfortunately, not one of the three Bruegels that Clovio cherished so faithfully can be located today.

Both Bruegel and Clovio beyond doubt were familiar with masterpieces of early book illumination and illustration, the field in which the art of miniature painting first developed and flourished. Even today there is a gemlike brilliance and a fascinating charm in the illuminated breviaries (prayer books) and books of hours that were prepared by early miniaturists for families of wealth and influence.

In such rich, radiant books, prized by aristocrats and art connoisseurs, scenes of farmwork and labor on the great estates were often shown in exquisite detail. Illustrations such as these deeply impressed Bruegel, and art historians have found significant similarity between Clovio's miniatures and the earliest among the surviving Bruegel paintings.

This reveals much about Bruegel's preferences and tastes. He was at last in Rome. Not many years before, Michelangelo had completed his tremendous and furious *Last Judgment*, covering one end wall of the Sistine Chapel in the Vatican. It blazed there, big, bold, full of anger and augury. Overhead, on the ceiling of the Sistine Chapel, were Michelangelo's frescoes with their imposing, idealized figures of characters in the great Biblical dramas. Even God himself was pictured in the instant of infusing life into Adam, ancestor of all mankind.

Yet Bruegel brought back to the Low Countries more artistic nourishment from the miniaturistic tradition, in which he found scope for his own special development, than from the powerful but tyrannical example of Michelangelo, whom so many other artists sought to follow, often to their own confusion and frustration.

The choice of the Tower of Babel as a subject is significant. It was not among the Biblical scenes that Michelangelo had placed on the Sistine ceiling. The theme had not very often been chosen by painters prior to this time, though some early miniaturists had placed it in their brilliant breviaries.

The Babel story in the Book of Genesis is brief and
dramatic. It tells of an early human plan to build a
tower reaching to heaven itself. This bold attempt
angered God. He cast on the tower builders, who until
then had spoken the same language, the curse of diverse
tongues. They were thus confused and confounded.
So the tower building ended in chaos, and the would-be
builders were scattered far over the earth, with their
new languages and misunderstandings.

The appeal of this stark, vivid, symbolic tale
remained with Bruegel after his return from Italy. It
bore fruit in two paintings, both of which survive today.
The better known of the two, signed and dated 1563, is
reproduced in color (plate i). Also, to illustrate the
different effects of two mediums that are both important
to Bruegel, an engraving based on that same painting
is shown here [47].

47   *The Tower of Babel*;
engraved by Antonio Prenner
c. 1728, after the painting
dated 1563 (Los Angeles)

Bruegel's concept is faithful both to the brief story in the Bible and to the engineering and architecture of his own time. He has created the monster tower as it might have been attempted in his native Low Countries in the sixteenth century rather than on the flat plain of Mesopotamia, the Biblical setting.

48 King Nimrod, detail of *The Tower of Babel*

At lower left stands a haughty monarch surrounded by guards, builders, stonemasons. He is King Nimrod, direct descendant of Noah—the same Nimrod to whom the Bible pays tribute as "a mighty hunter" and a "mighty one in the earth." His kingdom included Babel, which meant Babylon, and other regions of the Tigris and Euphrates valley, in what is now Iraq.

Nimrod's power is suggested by the workers bowing low before him. His overwhelming ambition is illustrated by the monster masonry structure that rises, level after level, until its unfinished top is wreathed in clouds!

This painting is praised deservedly for its precise picturing of the most advanced construction methods of the mid-sixteenth century. Many art historians have assumed that the tower was based on buildings that Bruegel had actually seen in Antwerp, Brussels, Amsterdam, and other Low Countries cities he is known to have visited. But in fact this multiple complex of arches within arches is closely similar to the interior construction of the great Colosseum of Rome erected in the first century A.D and still standing—perhaps the most familiar ruin in the Western world.

If this Babel painting and the interior construction plans of the Colosseum of Rome are compared, they provide convincing evidence that Bruegel knew how the great amphitheater had been built. He may even have brought sketches of its exposed skeleton back to the Low Countries in his notebooks.

The monster tower rises here above a large, active city. Houses, walls, and harbor cluster about the base. Ships and rafts are bringing building materials. Human workers swarm within and around the tower. Everywhere is activity and energy. One sees tiny hoists, scaffolding, and piles of stone and mortar.

The longer one looks at this abundant detail, the greater the feeling that just such a giant tower could have been built by men, and could even now be built, using Bruegel's picture as guide. Nothing is vague or ambiguous. It is actual, plausible, explicit—and exciting because of that.

Still another source out of the distant past may add to an understanding of how Bruegel arrived at his extraordinary design. The tower he painted is built with an inclined ramp or roadway spiraling around it from base to top. Eight levels of this ramp can be traced. And at the top, in the center of the tower, rises a still higher structure, not yet completed.

Why just this design? An answer can be found in a

49 Materials assembled at t[he] shore, detail of *The Tower of Babel*, engraving (page 74)

50 Central section of the Tower, detail of *The Tower of Babel*, engraving (page 74)

classic of Greek literature—the works of Herodotus, the great historian, travel-writer, and gossip-collector who lived in the fifth century B.C. Bruegel's painting follows the description of the ziggurat, or sacred tower, of Babylon, as given by Herodotus. He must have heard it from Babylonians who had seen that great tower while it yet stood, for it was destroyed, almost certainly, before Herodotus himself visited the site.

Herodotus wrote of "a tower of solid masonry, on which a second tower was raised, and on that a third, and so on, up to eight." He also spoke of an outside ramp or path: "The climb to the top is on the outside by a path that winds around all the towers."

Bruegel quite probably became familiar with Herodotus' description before he painted this Babel masterpiece. The tale of that tower attracted him because it was a great parable or allegory. He was constantly concerned with the pity and folly of human hatreds and conflicts. The tower of Babel story showed that once in the far past men spoke the same language, understood each other, and could work together. It was the kind of message most likely to attract this humane and thoughtful man. His *Tower of Babel* had meaning upon meaning, just as it had level upon level as it rose into the sky.

X *From Mountain Lands to Landscape Engravings*

51 Travelers, detail of *Alpine Landscape with Deep Valley*, engraving (page 80)

Bruegel's return journey to Antwerp took place in either 1553, 1554, or 1555, with the second date the most likely. He had wandered widely, enriching his memories and his notebooks with new vistas of magnificent mountain lands. Probably he headed north from Italy, possibly by way of Milan, entering Switzerland north of Lake Maggiore through the Giacomo Pass, near the juncture of the present cantons of Ticino and Valais.

Somewhat north and east of this mountain pass stands the peak of St. Gotthard, nearly seven thousand feet high. This was one of the many mountains that Bruegel swallowed with relish. An art treasure later owned by Rubens was a Bruegel picture of "Mount St. Goddard," which undoubtedly referred to this same peak. The picture is lost today, but not the indication of Bruegel's presence there as traveler and artist.

Scholars have carefully studied the body of Bruegel drawings, engravings, and paintings for other clues to his travels. There is, for example, a view of the valley of the Ticino River as seen from the Italian side between the Giacomo Pass and the slopes of St. Gotthard mountain. There is also a view called "Waltersspurg," which proves to be an old spelling for Waltensburg, in easternmost Switzerland, wedged between Austria, Italy, and tiny Liechtenstein.

One Bruegel sketch has been identified as that of a mountain near Innsbruck in the Austrian Tyrol, though it is surprising that he departed so far from the usual travel routes of his era.

The Belgian art historian Louis Lebeer has found in Bruegel's works traces of the region of Chillon, near Geneva, Switzerland. Very likely Bruegel passed through Geneva, then the stronghold of the religious reformer John Calvin, whose writings and followers were winning new adherents in the Low Countries.

Similarities to the countryside around Geneva have been traced in at least two of Bruegel's greatest paintings. In his famous *Harvesters* (plate IV) the shape of the distant lake and the contours of the plain resemble the view from the base of Mount Salève. Also parts of the great winter painting *Hunters in the Snow* (plate III) have been found to resemble certain vistas in the valley of the Rhone River.

Louis Lebeer has recognized several mountains—Mount Salève, Mount Catogne, and other peaks of the Savoy Range—in the famous series called the "Large Landscapes." These impressive and masterful prints were engraved by Jerome Cock himself from drawings supplied by Bruegel after his return to Antwerp. The originals must have been completed during the period 1555–58.

In all there were a dozen engravings in this series, plus a separate single print of even grander dimensions

52 Alpine Landscape with Deep Valley; engraved by Jerome Cock, after a drawing dated 1555 (Los Angeles)

called *The Great Alpine Landscape.* Jerome Cock
obviously recognized the power of his former apprentice's
designs.

Particular interest attaches to the print called
Alpine Landscape with Deep Valley [52]. Of the thirteen
engravings published following Bruegel's return to
Antwerp, this is the only one for which his original drawing survives today. That drawing is preserved, though
much damaged, in the great Louvre Museum, Paris,
and is sometimes called *Mountain Ravine.* It bears
the figures "55," indicating the date 1555.

Cock's engraving differs in various details from
Bruegel's original. The two rocks in the middle foreground of the engraving were added. Also many of the
human figures. Such changes show how an artist's
original concept might be altered during the engraving
process. Since Bruegel was at hand, we may assume
that he either agreed with or at any rate consented
to such alterations or additions.

Print lovers insist on the importance of the
participation of the original artist in the process of
reproduction, all the way to final printing from the
finished metal plates. The term "fine print," in fact,
is reserved for those that result from such collaboration.
Some of the great engravings based on Bruegel original
designs were not "fine prints" in this special sense,
for many were executed after his death.

A most striking difference appears when a finished
print is compared with the original drawing from
which it derives: each is a reversal, or mirror image,
of the other. Thus, in the *Alpine Landscape* print,
three heavily laden horses or mules are being driven up
the sloping road at *right* foreground. In the original
this takes place at *left*. Great birds that fly toward the
right in the print, fly left in the drawing. And so on.

This reversal is easily explained. The engraver
commonly placed the original design face upward on the
blank copperplate, with some suitable powder between
paper and metal. Then he traced major outlines by
means of a stylus; they were dim but sufficient to follow
as he dug into the blank metal with his burins.

Then when the completed copperplate was inked
and the damp paper was pushed against it in the
press, whatever stood at the left of the metal plate
would appear as a mark at the *right* of the printed paper,
and vice versa. In just the same way, if one stands

before a mirror and touches it with the right forefinger,
it will be met by what would be the left forefinger
of the reversed being in looking-glass-land!

This *Alpine Landscape* print is abundantly supplied
not only with scenery but also with human activities
and artifacts: houses, churches, castle, fortress, roads,
and so on. This is typical of Bruegel's treatment of great
landscape scenes. Also typical are two of his familiar
"trademarks"—the many birds flying across the sky
and the central importance given to the stream.

This cannot be considered a picture of one single
spot Bruegel saw during his travels, but rather a fusion,
a composite, of many. He combined diverse elements
into one whole, more varied, more dramatic, and
more abundantly active than would be likely in reality.

The spirit of this richly complex picture and of many
another by Bruegel suggests a statement in a poem,
"Boats in a Fog," by the American poet Robinson Jeffers:

> . . . *all the arts lose virtue*
> *Against the essential reality*
> *Of creatures going about their business*
>   *among the equally*
> *Earnest elements of nature.*

It was one of Bruegel's abundant virtues that his
art included this very reality: human creatures, and
animals, too, going about their tasks amidst the elements
of nature, represented earnestly and honestly.

It was reality of this sort that Bruegel mastered even
at a relatively early period in his work. Yet it was this
same Bruegel who, soon and suddenly afterward,
appeared also as a creator of wild, bizarre fantasies and
dreamlike symbols. Both Bruegels were superb, and
both were important parts of this extraordinarily
abundant and varied artist.

Jerome Cock, as publisher-engraver, and Peter
Bruegel, as inventor-designer, appreciated the value of
variety and human interest in a series such as this,
intended to appeal broadly. They found ways to avoid
sameness among the "Large Landscapes." Four of those
prints include figures from the Bible or Church history.

These figures, it is true, appear small and even
insignificant within the ample, craggy landscapes. But
they were mentioned in the titles. Their presence
permitted purchasers to relish the physical splendors of
this world while showing proper piety and respect

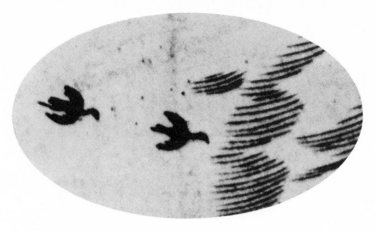

53 Birds, detail of *Alpine
Landscape with Deep Valley*,
engraving (page 80)

54 *Euntes in Emaus;* engraved
by Jerome Cock, after a
drawing c. 1558 (Los Angeles)

EVNTES IN EMAVS

for the religious creed so powerfully supported by the authorities and the Inquisition established by Emperor Charles V.

One of the prints with religious content is called *Euntes in Emaus* [54]. But for its title, one might assume it to be a purely secular landscape, composed of a Low Countries river at left, plus hills and a sheer cliff or two.

Emaus (now spelled Emmaus), however, is a small town near Jerusalem. According to Luke 24:13, it was on the way there that two disciples encountered Jesus after the Resurrection. Thus it was the scene of the recognition of "the risen Christ."

Three men in sixteenth century pilgrim garb can be seen under the noble tree to the right of center. The figure in the middle, his face turned entirely from us, shows a circular halo about his hat. This is Jesus, temporarily returned to the world. The other two, the disciples, still do not know his identity.

This takes place amidst houses and rural surroundings typical, but for the added cliffs and sheer hills, of the Campine and Brabant. The sun is sinking in the west. Cattle graze. Fishermen angle in the river. Horsemen ride their burdened steeds. Boatmen and sailors move their craft along the calm waters.

The world goes its accustomed and rather predictable way, unaware of the miraculous event under the tree. Melodrama is not only avoided, it is actually negated. The sacred is submerged in the secular. The wonder seems to be more in the richness and promise of man's world than in the miraculous event suggested by the title and hinted at so subtly in the drawing itself.

Another mingling of pious traditions and dramatic landscape composition is the print *S. Hieronymus in Deserto*, or *Saint Jerome in the Desert* [55]. In its plunge and sweep this vista is memorable. A pronounced diagonal, from lower left to upper right, divides the far away from the near. The distant triangle is definitely reminiscent of the Low Countries, a network of meandering streams on their way to the sea. And on the far horizon, many leaning sailing vessels and the buildings and tower of a sizable town may suggest Antwerp.

In great curves and ridges the hill at right rises to its summit, crowned by an extensive castle. At far right stands a stately tree, with wonderfully living foliage.

55 *St. Jerome in the Desert*;
engraving, after a drawing
of c. 1558 (Los Angeles)

Other trees, including evergreens, grow on the
slope below.

Only at the base of the nearest tree, his face hidden
by a great shade hat, can the "principal character"
be found. He sits, reading in complete concentration,
guarded by a faithful lion. Jerome traditionally was
served by lions in his desert hideaway.

This is indeed Bruegel's version of the famed Church
Father of the fourth century A.D., a cultured and
educated lover of the Latin and Greek classics who
repented and went to live in the desert near Antioch.
Once he had believed the style of the Hebrew Bible to be
crude; now he is determined to make it his model. So

he sits, studying the Old Testament, a halo about
his hat to signify his sainthood.

Jerome's sojourn in the barren desert was well
known. Yet Bruegel did not hesitate to offer this lush,
well-watered, and verdant scene, of mingled Low
Countries and Alpine parts, as the bleak desert whose
rigors the saint endured to mortify his pride and
purge his soul!

The abundant landscape is dotted and spotted with
figures of humans and animals. There are watchers,
wagons, teams of horses, boats of various kinds and
sizes. There are even two corpses hanging from a
gallows almost on the shore of the sea. Another gallows
frame nearby stands empty. Between the two gallows
rises a tall, dreadful wheel for punishment.

Birds fly in the sky where an intricate network of
clouds floats above the water-land complex below.
Rich variety and interest infuse this bleak and barren
desert of Chalcis near Antioch! It is almost as if Bruegel

*56 Village amid Woods, or
Pagus Nemorosus; engraving,
after a drawing of c. 1558
(Los Angeles)*

57 Team of horses and their driver, *From the Life*; pen and ink drawing, c. 1564 (Vienna)

with a sly smile were insisting on the contrast between that legendary parched desert and this fertile, well-worked, and well-populated land familiar to his fellow Flemings!

Other prints in the "Large Landscape" series include unobtrusive references to sacred stories. There are prints of the *Flight into Egypt*, showing Mary, Joseph, and the infant Jesus, and of the *Penitence* of Mary Magdalene.

There are also prints wholly rural, rather than religious, as indicated by their titles: *Nundinae Rusticorum*, which has to do with rural peddlers and merchants; *Insidiouses Auceps*, the cunning bird-catcher; and *Plaustrum Belgicum*, the Belgian wagon, looking much like the covered wagon one still finds on television. *Pagus Nemorosus*, or *Village amid Woods* [56] shows a scene wholly and solely of the Low Countries—flat, well wooded, so water-soaked that the covered wagon and its accompanying riders must "wade" as they ride past the village church, following the one and only road. Meanwhile, at the foot of the stately tree a rabbit feeds (lower right), and in the cloud-piled sky birds rise in splendid flight.

Bruegel managed to interweave much with his well-loved Low Countries waterways and the lively valleys, hills, cliffs, and crags that he had brought back from his Alpine excursions!

XI *Into Landscapes of the Human Heart*

58 Detail of *The Temptation of Saint Anthony,* engraving (page 91)

The "Large Landscapes" designed by Bruegel were successful. Master Bruegel, it would seem, might have continued for years doing similar assignments for Jerome Cock or other print publishers. In 1556, however, Bruegel's graphic output shifted suddenly into a very different direction—one that was both new and old.

The new pictures were in the fantastic and haunting manner of Hieronymus (Jerome) Bosch (1450–1516), that most original and baffling of artists. He had died years before Bruegel was born, so there was no personal contact between the two whose names were destined to be linked so often in art history. Yet Bosch had remained a strong influence. He was remembered especially for his wildly imaginative symbolic demons and monsters such as those in his *Temptation of St. Anthony* [59].

The first of Bruegel's prints in this vein, also a *Temptation of Saint Anthony* [60], was issued without his name. Publisher Cock clearly wanted his customers to think that it was an engraving after an original by the great Bosch himself. This was slightly misleading.

The original drawing was dated 1556, and the engraving was probably executed by Van der Heyden.

Underneath in Latin is a text that corresponds to lines in Psalm 34 (Psalm 33 in the version Bruegel used) of the Bible in English: "Many are the afflictions of the righteous [man]; but the Lord delivers him out of them all."

The righteous man here afflicted and tempted is Anthony. He is seated at lower right, apparently unaware of all the wild riots by demons and monsters around him. Radiance shines above his head. A sacred book lies before him. As he reads, his mind remains firm against distraction or despair.

The infernal fantasies around him are both complex and cryptic. Most of these symbols may have been understandable to imaginative Flemings in the sixteenth century, but understandable or not, they were assuredly fascinating—and so they remain today. Such symbols supplied the link to Hieronymous Bosch, who has well been called "perhaps the greatest master of fantasy who ever lived." Bosch had indeed been more original, unusual, and independent than any previous artist. Some artists who followed him had worked in ways that recalled his style, but none before Bruegel had so powerfully adapted his essentials and expanded them.

An art puzzle lies here. Why did Bruegel draw and Cock publish such an agitated fantasy in a style dating back forty or fifty years? In fact, its roots reached even further into the past, for Bosch had himself drawn on images, symbols, and patterns derived from the Middle Ages.

Could it be that by 1556 it had become safer to attribute some of these caustic symbols to a dead master than to a living artist such as Peter Bruegel?

Conditions in the Low Countries surely had stimulated increased interest in the demonic fantasies of Bosch. There were growing troubles and tensions, wars, religious conflicts, the Inquisition, heavy taxes, Spanish interference with traditional liberties of the Low Countries—all this, and threats of worse to come.

Many of the symbols in this Bruegel *Temptation of Saint Anthony* are obscure, yet one senses clearly enough that it represents a deplorable or even catastrophic condition of affairs. Ruin, fire, conflict are everywhere. So general are the symptoms of downfall and decay that the saint's sublime indifference may make him seem more like a fool than a philosopher.

This print powerfully suggests that things are rotten in both Church and State. Thus, at the center appears a monstrous turbaned head, topped by a huge decaying fish, within which men battle to the death. A tree projects from the mouth of the fish, a flag flying from its branches. From the flag dangle two seals such as those attached to the decrees or "bulls," issued by the Pope in Rome.

Dr. Adriaan J. Barnouw, an authority on the history and culture of the Low Countries, declared that the reference here is to "the papacy, the source of corruption

59 Hieronymus (Jerome) Bosch, *The Temptation of Saint Anthony*; engraving published by Jerome Cock (Washington)

60 Peter Bruegel the Elder, *The Temptation of Saint Anthony*; engraving, dated 1556, after a drawing of c. 1556 (New York)

MVLTÆ TRIBVLATIONES IVSTORVM DE OMNIBVS iis LIBERABIT EOS DOMINVS· PSAL· 33·

MVLTÆ TRIBVLATIONES IVSTORVM, DE OMNIBVS IIS LIBERABIT EOS DOMINVS· PSAL· 33

within the body of the Church." The tree sprouting
from the head of this fish, he saw, however, as a
suggestion of "new life" for the Church.

In the distance a church building is ablaze. The
horrible head on which the Church-fish rests is sinking
in the waters. One eye of the head is formed like a
broken window. Its tongue is a mass of fire and smoke.
A pair of spectacles penetrates one nostril. This head
stands for the State, or government. Clearly it is in
a desperate plight.

Still other symbols indicate how timely such a picture
must have appeared to educated citizens of the Low
Countries. At the left, back of the sinking State-head,
a swollen domelike object floats on the waters. From
an arched opening within it, multitudes of soldiers
stream out. The Oriental appearance of the object
suggests the formidable Turks who were then menacing
Europe from the east and south.

This nightmarish print is believed to be Bruegel's
earliest design in the Bosch manner. It shows abundant
imagination and power in the direction of what Vasari,
in his *Lives of the Painters*, called "fantasies, dreams,
and other imaginations." No wonder both Bosch
and Bruegel are looked on as forerunners of the recent
artistic style called surrealism, in which dreamlike
elements are so basic!

The *Saint Anthony* print must have been acclaimed,
for Jerome Cock hastened to follow it with other
Four Winds publications in a similar style. During 1556
Bruegel prepared at least three more such designs,
all engraved and then published by Cock during the
next year, 1557.

When the drawing illustrating the proverb *Big Fish
Eat Little Fish* [61], engraved by Van der Heyden,
was first published by Cock in print form, it not only
lacked Bruegel's name but actually had Bosch's added!
It is possible that Bruegel based his design in part
on some ideas he found in Bosch; but the switch of
names seems to have been one more effort by Cock to
benefit by a current enthusiasm for Bosch. From
this time on, however, Bruegel's own name appeared on
the engravings made from his originals, even in the
most Boschlike style.

Fantasy, morality, and warnings combine here. "The
big fish eat the little" was a familiar Flemish proverb,
resembling the English expression "Dog eat dog,"

to describe cutthroat competition between people in commerce, in careers, and in social life. The message is the same as Jonathan Swift's when he wrote:

So, naturalists observe, a flea,
Hath smaller fleas on him that prey;
And these have smaller fleas to bite 'em
And so proceed ad infinitum.

Such a pictorial message and moral must have seemed most timely. During this period, especially in the Antwerp metropolis, ruinous competitions and speculative crises were frequent. Unemployment and acute distress existed side by side with great wealth and windfall profits. More and more sharply man appeared in the terrible role of wolf to man.

In this drawing the superfish, slit open, releases a flood of smaller fish he has swallowed. These, in turn, disgorge still other and smaller prey. It is an object lesson in the outcome of unlimited competition, a

61 Big Fish Eat Little Fish; pen and ink drawing, dated 1556 (Vienna)

62 *Avarice*, or *Avaritia*;
pen and ink drawing, dated
1556 (London)

fantasy of greed-and-grab. Such is the moral pointed
out by a father for the guidance of his child, in the
rowboat at the bottom.

Fantastic monsters infest the scene. At right, a fish
with human legs walks up the bank, a small fish in
his mouth. In the sky flies a fish with snake tail and
insect wings. Near the stern of the rowboat a great clam
seeks to devour a fish which is in the act of swallowing
a smaller fish. And so on, and on, without rest or mercy.

A military figure saws into the belly of the monster
fish with a toothed knife. The "trademark" on the
blade is a symbol that stands for the world—man's
sinful, spiteful, topsy-turvy world, so opposed to the
righteousness of the heavenly kingdom.

This is a far cry from the art of drawing or painting
elegant nudes in the manner of Italian Renaissance

masters. Bruegel has here sought intensity of meaning rather than beauty of physical form.

Another Bruegel drawing of 1556 deserves a place of major importance in his abundant graphic contributions. It is called *Avarice* (*Avaritia* in Latin) [62], and it launched the world-famous cycle of drawings-into-engravings known as Bruegel's "Seven Deadly Sins."

During the following year Bruegel made designs also for the other six sins: *Pride, Envy, Anger, Gluttony, Lust* or *Unchastity*, and *Sloth*. All were engraved by Van der Heyden and published by Cock at the Four Winds, with outstanding success. Fortunately the world today still has the original drawings as well as fine prints from the engravings of all seven "Sins."

A single pattern underlies the composition of each, combining allegory, demonic symbolism, and everyday realities. The pattern appears clearly here in *Avarice*. In the center foreground sits the female "queen." She personifies the sin. In front of her is her mascot or pet —the animal symbol of that sin—in this case a toad, considered in Flemish folklore to be so avaricious that it fed on dirt or sand!

Queen Avarice holds a lapful of money, and reaches for more into a treasure chest which a monstrous attendant fills from a broken jug.

In the strange, hellish landscape are groups of humans. These are the slaves or addicts of the sin. Among them are symbolic demons, some of whom provide suitable torments for the humans.

Back of the queen we see a stout moneylender or pawnbroker taking a poor man's plate. Meanwhile, above him, a thief reaches into the roof to steal the money hoarded there. A demon-bird pecks at the thief. From the rotting shack of the moneylender project gigantic shears in which the broken body of a human victim is caught. Below and to the right, a demon points out this grisly example to two terrorized humans.

On the other side of the shack, despairingly seated on the ground, two sinners look at a tally sheet. The winged demon beside them presents this reckoning, which they are clearly unable to pay.

To the left and above, a group of crossbowmen are shooting at a target. Appropriately, it is a purse, from which money leaks. One shooter, wearing monklike garb, is being robbed of his own purse by two young thieves behind him.

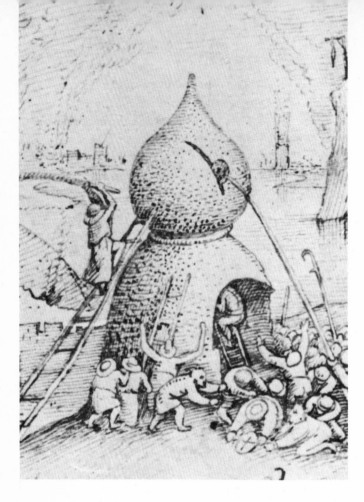

63 Coin bank, detail of
Avarice (page 94)

On the opposite side, near the right margin, a strange
domed structure, a Flemish "piggy-bank" by its shape,
is invaded by an army of tormented addicts of Avarice.
They try to pull down a coin about to go into the
slot on top. One, with upraised club, stands on a ladder,
about to break open this receptacle.

As one might expect in Bruegel's world, fire is at
work. A fantastic building burns nearby. And in the sky
flies a giant inflated fish with insect wings and spiky tail.

In the foreground at left crouch horrible monsters.
Their distorted forms symbolize and mock the sin. A
squatting beggar holds a bowl with but one coin.
A nightmare head-with-legs wears as hat a sort of
swollen purse that drags in the dirt.

The abundance and interconnection of symbols
pictured in all these "Sins" are greater than can be
analyzed here. Each of the drawings manages, with its
haunting images and incidents, to convey Bruegel's own
idea of human sin—an idea psychologically mature and
surprisingly modern. Briefly, he did not follow the
medieval idea of sin as something into which

unsuspecting humans were tricked or trapped hopelessly by malignant devils. Sin, rather, was the result of human egotism, ignorance, and folly. Hence, it could be cured—by educating humans.

Meanwhile, so long as sin persisted, the sinner was punished—by the consequences of the sin itself. One could invert the old saying that "Virtue is its own reward," and affirm that "Sins provide their own punishments."

No black magic is at work here. The devils are all symbolical, not actual. Bruegel did not visualize a personal, physical Devil, like the sinister being at whom Martin Luther said he had once thrown an inkwell. Bruegel, even in treating the many-centuries-old theme of the mortal or deadly sins, was forward-looking, rather than a captive of old attitudes.

The masterful original design drawing for the sin of *Sloth* [64] and also the print made from the engraving

64 *Sloth*, or *Desidia*; pen and ink drawing, dated 1557 (Vienna)

SEGNITIES ROBVR FRANGIT, LONGA OCIA NERVOS
Traecheyt maeckt machteloos en verdrooeft Die fennwen dat de menfch medwers toe en dooeht

65   *Sloth*, or *Desidia*; engraved
by Peter van der Heyden,
1558 (Los Angeles)

66   Detail of *Sloth*

[65] by Van der Heyden, published in 1558, make clear the differences as well as the similarities of the two media.

Queen Sloth lies asleep or in a stupor. Her elbow rests on her animal mascot or "totem," the slothful donkey. Below her feet Bruegel placed the Latin word *Desidia*, standing for sloth of the most deadly and depressing sort—extreme apathy.

Though each of the "Sins" shows its own special symbols, certain symbols are repeated several times in different pictures. Thus, hollowness—whether a hollow tree, a broken house, or a shattered egg—stands for degeneration and decay, moral rather than merely physical.

The weird, unnatural combining of animal parts into impossible monsters, insect-bird-fish-mammal pieces all scrambled together, also stands for moral disruption and unnatural evils, as well as portraying demonic creatures.

Other haunting symbols abound in *Sloth*. The background clock, with its single human "hand," points to the late hour of eleven. The bell-ringer sounds the alarm in the tree. The slimy snail and the monstrous slug slide through the mountain rocks. Humans drown in the stream of sin. Owls, birds of evil, brood. It is an intricate network of symbol and secret sign. What one cannot read clearly one can often sense emotionally. The degradation and slavery of the sinful man or woman are unforgettably implied.

Bruegel, in turning from rural and mountain landscapes to the wildernesses of the human heart, had to find new images, new combinations, new relationships between shape and substance. He was guided in part by the pioneer work of Bosch, but to a large extent he created his own language of symbols.

XII *Further Follies and Difficult Virtues*

67 Detail of *Hope*, engraving (page 108)

For Bruegel 1558 to 1562 was an important transition period. He discovered and developed new and powerful ways to picture the world around him and to express many of the most critical and enlightened ideas of his time.

One example is his design of 1558, called *Elck* or *Everyman* [68]. Probably engraved by Van der Heyden, it was published first by Cock in the form shown here. Later a new edition, with several inscriptions added, was published by Joan Galle.

A bearded bespectacled man, at center, searches among piles of possessions, scattered like junk around him. He holds a lantern, though it is not night. That man is at the same time searching in at least four other places. He appears in a barrel at lower right, in a sack at upper left, and below, in an open basket or hamper. Finally, at the upper right, he engages in a futile tug-of-war with a younger, more determined man.

This old man who cannot find what he seeks, despite spectacles and lantern, is Everyman, or Bruegel's fellow man, or—in fact—all of us!

What is his multiple, unrewarded search? The engraving from this drawing suggests the interpretation in verses in three languages: Flemish, French, and Latin. The Latin says sternly: "There is no one who does not everywhere seek for his own advantage, no one who does not seek himself in everything he does, no one who does not strive at all times for his personal gain; this one tugs, that one tugs, all have the same craving to possess."

A free poetic interpretation suggests the direction in which the Flemish and French verses tend:

Always, each man is seeking for himself alone—
And everywhere. . . . So how can one stay lost?
Each man will pull and tug, and grunt and groan,
Seeking to get more for himself—get most!

And no man knows himself, despite such seeking;
No light will help him in this lonely place.
Strange! Though he looks with eyes forever open,
He never sees at last his own true face.

Near the top of the drawing, just right of center, hangs a poster or picture depicting a man gazing into a hand mirror. The Flemish motto below declares, *"No one knows himself."*

The things scattered around the scene suggest Bruegel's satire. They include: bales of merchandise, packed for shipment; an account book; a scale such as bankers and moneylenders used to weigh coins; playing cards, among which the five of diamonds can be distinguished; dice, and other gambling devices. To the

68　*Elck*, or *Everyman*; pen and ink drawing, dated 1558 (London)

69 The old man searches everywhere but cannot find what he seeks; details of *Elck*

70 The alchemist (below) and his wife and children; details of *The Alchemist*

wealthy speculators and merchant-adventurers
gathered from the wide world in Antwerp, this satirical
message must have been clear enough!

Soldiers and officers are encamped in the
background, at the upper left, their banners billowing
in the wind. War is under way or in preparation. Rulers
and nations, no less than private persons, are seeking
profit, gain, and advantage at the expense of others.

The drawing of the *Alchemist* [71], made by
Bruegel in 1558, was later engraved by Philip Galle and
published by Cock.

Like *Everyman*, it includes within one picture actions
that take place at different times. The main picture
shows a last desperate effort of the rabid and ragged
alchemist (at right) to discover a method that will
transform base metals into gold. Through the window,
upper left, lies the future, or final, outcome: the same
alchemist, his wife, and neglected children are all on
their way to the poorhouse.

To make this sequence quite clear, Bruegel places in
the main picture one child (top center) wearing an

71 *The Alchemist*; pen and
nk drawing, dated 1558
(Berlin)

earthenware pot as he plays, neglected and dirty, in the
cupboard. The same pot is still on the child's head in
the scene of final pauperization through the window.

This is art that tells an anecdote or story. Yet
Bruegel has avoided sentimentalism and cheap tricks.
Obviously Bruegel detested the superstitions and taint
of magic that underlay so many of the alchemist's
efforts. He took pains to make his disapproval perfectly
clear. Beside the ragged alchemist manipulating his
retorts and beakers, his wife holds the empty family
purse. His crazy assistant wears a fool's cap as he
manipulates the bellows.

At left sits the sage commentator, or voice of
experience. He is the scholar who literally points up the
moral, for his finger leads us to an open book before
him. Its pages carry the Flemish heading ALGHE MIST,
which means "all rubbish." It is, of course, a pun,
suggesting by sound that the costly efforts of the
ALCHE MIST are all worthless and wasted.

Bruegel here shows familiarity with the substances
used in such attempts to attain wealth. He has labeled
cans and sacks around the room with Flemish names
such as *drogery* (drugs) and *sulfer*.

The miserable and desperate state of the alchemist
himself, the confusion and chaos in his house, reveal
how far he has persisted in this fruitless search. His
unkempt head is outlined against a great earthenware
still. On the board above his head is tacked his current
recipe or formula for transforming lead or iron into gold.
It bears alchemical and astrological symbols. To
Bruegel, whose viewpoint was surprisingly scientific for
his time, this has all been a recipe for disappointment
and ruin, for misery and humiliation.

No demons or monsters appear in *The Alchemist*.
The humans in this tragedy are real and recognizable
enough. They are the victims of ignorance and greed.

The prints of "Seven Deadly Sins" obviously were
a great success for publisher Cock. Now his resourceful
designer Bruegel began drawings for a different but
parallel cycle, to be known, logically enough, as the
"Seven Cardinal Virtues." During 1559 drawings were
completed for four of the seven, including the familiar
trio *Faith*, *Hope* and *Charity*, plus one more, *Prudence*.

This cycle of the "Seven Virtues" showed a new,
more realistic, restrained approach. They are allegorical

pictures, and by no means "photographic," for they
bring together on one sheet of paper a wide variety of
human situations and activities. Six of the seven contain
no dreamlike fantasies, no demons or monsters, not
even angels. Only in *Fortitude* do diabolical creatures
appear, representing the deadly sins that are resisted so
stoutly.

The mood of the "Virtues" is sober, even somber.
There is an implied irony, as if the pictures were
saying: "Here is what men in our society regard as
Faith—or Justice—or Charity. What a sad spectacle!"

Before discussing the "Virtues" in greater detail,
it may be helpful to look at some of the influences
that may have affected Bruegel. These same influences
seem to have been at work also in his "Sins" series.

Two men in particular are important to the shaping
of Bruegel's ideas at this period. One, a remarkable
thinker, writer, reformer, and engraver named Dirk
Volckertszoon Coornhert (1522–1590), became the outstanding champion of religious tolerance in the Low
Countries and even served time in prison for his liberal
religious views.

The other was the great printer, Christopher Plantin,
head of the Golden Compass shop. A French-born
resident of Antwerp, he was destined to become one of
its most remembered citizens.

Both men were members of the "House of Love,"
a fraternal and philosophical group whose ideas closely
paralleled those expressed in the pictures and captions
for Bruegel's "Seven Sins" and "Seven Virtues."
They emphasized tolerance and rejected narrow theo-
logical dogmas or rigid rituals.

Coornhert, a notably cultured and creative man,
wrote on philosophical and ethical subjects. He was a
musician, an able fencer, a competent copper engraver.
Indeed, through his many translations of poetry and
prose, he helped to mold a literary Dutch language for
the future. His tolerant, liberal ideas, though they
seem reasonable enough today, were unorthodox and
even dangerous in his time. Bruegel, always drawn to the
intellectually advanced and liberal minds around him,
appears to have reflected these views in his work.

Plantin, for a time head of the "House of Love"
group in Antwerp, endured religious persecution, too,
and at one period was forced to hide in Paris for a
year. His house in Antwerp was a gathering place for

notable humanists, geographers, musicians, and writers.
Like Coornhert, he combined manual work skills
with far-reaching culture and education.

Bruegel at this time had begun to act as a kind of
artistic bridge between the pictorial heritage of the
Middle Ages and the new, expansive, humane, scientific,
and forward-looking attitudes of men like Coornhert
and Plantin. Both medieval and modern elements
can be traced in Bruegel's masterpieces.

Hope suggests optimism, but that is not the aspect
depicted in Bruegel's print *Hope* [72]. Designed in
1559, it was engraved by the burins of Philip Galle.

Here is a veritable "sea of troubles" in which Hope
stands calmly on a great anchor, holding in her hands
the peasant's spade and sickle. A beehive forms her
hat. It was a truism of the Middle Ages that peasants
and sailors were most dependent on hope, for they

72 *Hope,* or *Spes;* engraved
by Philip Galle, after a drawi[
dated 1559 (Washington)

LVCVNDISSIMA   EST   SPEI   PERSVASIO,   ET   VITAE   IMPRIMIS
NECESSARIA,   INTER   TOT   AERVMNAS   PENEQ   INTOLERABILES.

always faced disaster from unfavorable weather.

The Latin proverb below provides a key to this assemblage of misfortunes: "Most pleasant is the assurance that hope gives us, and most essential to existence, among so many almost intolerable woes."

On sea and on land such woes are abundantly illustrated: shipwrecks, drownings, floods, fire, imprisonment, hard labor on the soil, risky voyages on the ocean.

Such is the human condition—or at least the condition of a large part of humanity. The abounding woes are menacing, terrible, almost intolerable.

Hope persists amidst all this misery, making life possible to endure. And where liberty is lost, as in the prison tower at left, the shackled prisoners express their hope by folding their hands in prayer. A pair of prisoners are lowering a jug from the barred upper window, perhaps seeking water to drink. Right of the jug perches another prisoner: the captive falcon, hoping to have its hood removed.

Many a small but significant detail emphasizes the extremity of peril. At right the men in the sinking vessel are so frightened that their hair seems to stand on end. In the distant sky, top right, a crescent moon suggests that these multiple catastrophes are taking place at night.

This is truly the most somber side of human hope. It is not hope for wealth, for honor, or even for a lucky fall of the dice in a gambling game. It is hope merely for survival in the face of threatening extinction.

Another remarkable and revealing picture in the

"Virtues" cycle is *Justice* as engraved by Philip Galle
[74]. Allegorical Justice stands blindfolded, bearing
her sword of authority and her scales of equity, amidst
an extraordinary assemblage of punishments and legal
murders involving hundreds of condemned men, magis-
trates, executioners, torturers, and bystanders gathered
to see it all done.

The blindfold is supposed to prove that Justice
does not recognize or respect persons in her even-handed
application of the law. As one probes deeper into
this great pictorial record of man's inhumanity to man,
one may come to suspect that Justice prefers not to
see all that is done in her name!

Shocking things are taking place. Yet these were not
"cruel and unusual punishments" for the 1550's.
There is no reason to suspect Bruegel of trying to be
sadistic. Some commentators regard this as a tremendous
and hidden satire on grim realities of his era.

In Latin, below, stand the dark words that set the
tone for the whole: "The law's aim is either through
punishment to correct the person punished, or by
his example to improve others, or by overcoming the
evil to protect the generality [society]."

Into a great porch and courtyard, Bruegel has
marshaled the machinery of established legal justice. At
right stands a judge, bearing in his hand a chastising
rod, as he sentences two unkempt prisoners who
stand before him. The crucifix that has been pressed
into the hand of one reveals that it must be the extreme
penalty—death—which is being decreed.

At left, about halfway up the picture, a headsman
swings his sword to decapitate a condemned man, while
somewhat to the right a priest prays for his soul.

Through the twin arches at upper right, convicted
thieves are about to have their right hands cut off.
This was a common punishment in the period.

Outside the stairs at left, a convicted man tied to a
stake is being lashed with a bundle of sharp branches.
Another such torture-tool is ready to use when
the first wears out.

A poor devil, his hands and feet tied together behind
him, is hoisted high to swing and suffer close beside
the stone walls of the building.

Farther still, a convicted heretic is being burned
alive amidst a great upbillowing of smoke and a
concourse of spectators, both on foot and on horseback.

SCOPVS LEGIS EST AVT VT EV̄ QVĒ PVNIT EMENDET, AVT POENA
EIVS CAETEROS MELIORES REDDET AVT SVBLATIS MALIS CAETERI SECVRIORES VIVAT.

74 *Justice*, or *Iusticia*;
engraved by Philip Galle, after
a drawing dated 1559
(Washington)

The Inquisition has done its fiery work here!

The horizon, as in so many Bruegel pictures from
this time until his death, sprouts a ghastly crop of
gallows, gibbets, and wheels. Bodies hang in pairs on
two of the gallows. On three of the six terrible wheels
headless bodies of victims are exposed.

However, it is in the left foreground that Bruegel
offers the most striking, and for modern times shocking,
illustration of human justice in action. A prisoner
lies stretched on a rack, now being twisted to extend his
tormented limbs. He is being "questioned." This is
a police third degree to the nth power! At the same time
a torturer holds a torch from which he carefully drips
hot pitch onto the victim's limbs!

This is no unofficial outrage or atrocity perpetrated
in the heat of passion. The stout examining magistrate
is there, with his thorned stick of authority, dictating

to the clerk the results of the examination. Everywhere is evidence of approved red tape and protocol.
All that is done is in order—the kind of order
sanctioned by the ruling powers of the era.

Whipping, torture, burning, killing—all this was in
the machinery of justice as Bruegel revealed it. One
more small but essential detail is shown close to the
extreme upper-left corner: a great crucifix stands on a
hill overlooking the place of execution. Adriaan
Barnouw, who loved the art of Bruegel, has pointed
out that this is "the Cross of Christ." Its presence
"above this scene of woe" is a "guarantee that justice
thus administered has the sanction of the Supreme
Judge. For its aim is not revenge but the improvement
and protection of society."

In 1560 Bruegel completed designs for the two final
"Virtues," *Fortitude* and *Temperance* [75]. In *Fortitude*,
as noted, he returned to the use of demonic beasts
and monsters in the Boschlike style.

More significant here, however, is Bruegel's surprising interpretation of temperance as shown in the
engraving of this name. It tells us much about the
artist's world and his attitudes toward it. Temperance
for Bruegel is the sum total of human arts, sciences,
and worthwhile intellectual activities. In other words, it
is the opposite of excess, of time-wasting, of barbarism,
and of ignorance.

Temperance herself is a strange figure, encumbered
by many devices for purposeful discipline and useful,
productive labor. A horse's bit rests between her teeth
and the reins are in her own right hand. The other
hand holds a pair of spectacles. In short, she controls
herself, and observes closely. On her head is a clock,
the regulator of man's useful labors by day or night.
Underfoot lies the blade of a windmill, which harnesses
for drainage or grinding grain the otherwise untamed
force of the wild winds.

Her belt is a knotted snake, perhaps suggesting her
mastery over physical desires that might otherwise
disrupt human civilization. It is, indeed, "civilization,"
in the best sense of the term, that Bruegel summarizes
here. This is quite different from the narrower
meaning that the word temperance usually has in
English—meaning merely the avoidance of excesses in
drinking or eating.

VIDENDVM, VT NEC VOLVPTATI DEDITI PRODIGI ET LVXVRIOSI
APPAREAMVS, NEC AVARA TENACITATI SORDIDI AVT OBSCVRI EXISTAMVS

75 *Temperance*, or *Temperantia*; engraved by Philip Galle, after a drawing dated 1560 (Washington)

Beginning at lower right and proceeding counter-clockwise to lower left are groups of people whose activities represent, in succession: (1) grammar or letters; (2) dialectic, speech, or debate; (3) geometry, or earth measurements; (4) astronomy, or celestial measurements; (5) rhetoric, or drama; (6) music, both instrumental and vocal; and (7) arithmetic, including the painter's art, which involves harmonious proportions.

1) Grammar is a school, taught by a seated master at far right. A child before him is learning his *a-b-c*'s.

2) Half a dozen learned and pious men are disputing. According to one commentator, Romdahl, they include spokesmen for the principal religious groups then found actually, if not legally, in the Low Countries. Farthest right, in robe and brimless cap, is a Catholic. The bearded man beside him is a Jewish rabbi. The three others are, or may be, spokesmen for different

Protestant groups. A sixth man, whose face appears between priest and rabbi, is not identified.

The Bible remains closed on the stand behind them. It has been suggested that Bruegel here hinted at the view taken by the so-called Libertine or Spiritual groups such as the "House of Love": that true religion should be found in the Scriptures rather than in the polemics of the rival theologians. But these arguing creed-supporters are paying no attention to the Bible!

3) The uses of geometry are clearly shown. With plumb line and compass two men measure a standing pillar. Right of them can be seen artillery and crossbow. The trajectories of their missiles are calculated by means of geometry. Lower, to the left of the base of the column, are other instruments for measuring angles and positions. A stonemason works on a slab on which a sculptor has engraved a figure in relief. In the distance, the boundaries of a farm are being fixed by means of geometry.

4) Near top center appears a bold concept: a huge globe of the earth, its equator banded. A geographer uses a large compass to measure distance on the globe, while on its top an astronomer boldly seeks to

76 Details of *Temperance*, engraving (page 113)

take the measure of the moon. Stars spangle the sky, and the sun glows bright at left. By this time, Bruegel was acquainted either with leading geographers, cartographers, and men of science themselves, or with their ideas.

5) The performing arts are in action at upper left. Three actors appear on an elevated stage before a standing audience. Their play, like this entire engraving, is an allegory. The Fool peers around the corner at right. The young actor in noble garb is said to represent Hope, and in fact in the drawing the word "Hope" appeared lettered on his cloak. The gesturing lady is said to represent Faith. At extreme left, behind her, a prompter can be seen through the parted curtain.

A flag above the stage bears the symbol for the world, upside down, suggesting topsy-turvy relationships, and perhaps that "All the world's a stage. . . . " Still higher crouches the theatrical propman and herald, holding a horn with which to announce new acts or supply sound effects.

6) At least four different kinds of music widely popular in Bruegel's day are shown here. There is an organ for church music, a choral group mingling young and old male voices, an instrumental ensemble behind; and on the floor a lute and harp for worldly instrumental music. Even the bellows-pumper is provided to give pressure for the organ.

7) At lower left, three people are reckoning accounts, money exchanges, and other arithmetic tasks. The fur-hatted woman appears to depend on crude country-style reckoning, performed on the smooth board of a bellows. The hatless man beside her draws neat Arabic numerals. The rich merchant wears a hat and lays out his coins as he consults his account books.

Finally, at far left, his back completely turned on these money matters, we see a painter at his easel. Bruegel did not neglect his own art and high calling!

A visual survey such as this could have been conceived and executed only by an artist attuned to the intellectual life of his times. He was a man of culture, subtlety, refinement, with abounding love for the best in life, though with no illusions about life's trials and difficulties.

Temperance displays Bruegel's piling up of examples to illustrate a meaningful theme. In his paintings also appear many instances of such pictorial elaboration.

XIII Paintings of Multiplicity and Darker Moods

77 Detail of *The Battle Between Carnival and Lent*; oil on wood panel (page 118)

Wonderfully varied in content, style, and significance, Bruegel's finest and most famous paintings were done between 1559 and 1568. He did not cease to make great drawings during this decade of final fulfilment, but more and more his color paintings came to overshadow even his wonderful output of graphic art.

During 1559–62 Bruegel continued to live and work in Antwerp. These four years fall into two parts: the mood and style of his exuberant principal paintings of 1559–60, and in sharp contrast, the bitter, somber works associated with the years 1561–62.

Two crowded canvases of 1559 initiate what might be called the "multipaintings" of Peter Bruegel the Elder: *The Battle Between Carnival and Lent* [78] and *The Netherlandish Proverbs*.

Carnival stands for *carne-vale*, or "Farewell, meat!" It ushers in the season of Lenten self-denial and repentance. The theme of Bruegel's well-populated painting is, in fact, the mocking of the piety and sour-faced restraint of Lent by the carousing champions of Carnival.

This allegorical contest fills an authentic Flemish town square with about a hundred and seventy people of all ages, sizes, conditions, and activities. Their symbolic leaders face each other at front center: at left fat King Carnival carries as lance a great spit piercing a roasted pig; at right Lady Lent, a lean hag, projects her wooden paddle bearing two meager herrings!

From the church at upper right marches a pious Lenten procession. From the opposite side strut the Carnival merrymakers, flaunting their pleasures of the flesh. Each of these scores of individuals does something specific and significant. They engage in games, gambolings, mummeries, mockeries, pranks, and

78   *The Battle Between Carnival and Lent;* oil on wood panel, signed and dated 1559 (Vienna)

pious observances. The picture is swarming, alive, urgent, complex—yet not confused. The eye, fascinated, returns to it again and again, ever making new discoveries.

Nothing quite like this had ever before been attempted or attained. Italian masters had painted multifigure compositions, all quite carefully and harmoniously composed, correct, fluent, ingenious, and —usually—quite artificial in effect. Bruegel, working far closer to caricature than to idealization, spreads here a broad and colorful social spectrum: plausible, solid people, social beings, set in a real urban environment, not in some classic utopian framework. The effect is one of abundant, sweeping life and enormous richness.

The Flemish Proverbs, another great multipainting of 1559, sets side by side, in a single realistic but artificially assembled scene, groups of figures that enact between seventy-five and eighty-five different proverbs and folksayings of that era. The picture is exceptional, not only for its bold use of color, but as a kind of "charade" showing what Bruegel's fellow-Flemings said about common problems of everyday living. The proverbs thus illustrated are not stated in any written text on the painting. Many of them, however, have been identified by scholars.

Another multiple masterpiece is Bruegel's *Children's Games* of 1560 (plate II and detail on pages 26–27).

In a Flemish village, children by the hundreds are playing familiar games and pastimes of the period. At least eighty different games have been recognized. Bruegel himself probably had played or watched them all.

Some of the games are familiar today: rolling hoops, leapfrog, gymnastics, tumbling, top-spinning, hide-and-seek, and so on. Others remain difficult to identify, even for modern Belgians of the Antwerp and Brussels regions. Children's games, though persistently handed on from one generation to the next, apparently do change during the centuries!

These painted amusements are, however, all authentic and natural. None needs any aids more complex than a bench, a fence, a ball to throw, or a top to spin. And all this wealth of activity is fitted into an authentic Flemish locale, within a panel area of less than 37 by 64 inches!

In the Low Countries at this time resentments and resistance against many of the policies of the new ruler, Philip II of Spain, continued to grow.

A new peace treaty in the spring of 1559 halted fighting in the repeated wars between Spain and France. Troops of the Spanish monarch, however, including many brutal German mercenaries, were kept garrisoned in the Low Countries, and were feared and resented by the residents. The States-General, as the only body representing the seventeen provinces of the Low Countries, asked Philip to withdraw these troops, but they remained until two years later.

Philip prepared a number of schemes to control the Low Countries in line with his royal policies. He intended to rule them from afar, for he was eager to return to Spain.

He secured the Pope's approval to redistribute the Low Countries church districts, or dioceses, which were presided over by bishops. More than a dozen additional dioceses were carved out of the old, enraging many nobles, abbots, and some of the former bishops. The common people, too, were resentful and apprehensive. They feared that the new bishops, appointed only if acceptable to Philip, would serve as agents of the hated Inquisition. Philip appeared, once again, to be manipulating the Church to serve his own political ends. Increasingly, Flemings and Hollanders alike saw themselves as pawns of the policies of a Spanish monarch alien to their language and traditions, and stubbornly determined to infringe their liberties while taxing them heavily.

Philip's firm attachment to the Inquisition became clear enough in 1559, when he cautioned his half-sister, Margaret of Parma, now installed in Brussels as "governess" of the Low Countries, to be tireless in enforcing the edicts (placards) against heretics. Then he left, never again to return.

In the Low Countries, widespread relief greeted the departure of the gloomy, formal, and sanctimonious Philip. Many native nobles and men of affairs hoped that, with Philip and his entourage safely in Spain, it would be possible to make Margaret of Parma see things their way. But events soon showed that they were in many instances both overoptimistic and incautious. Nevertheless, the 1559 mood of relief, hope, and expansion of spirit may be reflected in Bruegel's memorable multipaintings of that period.

Religious terror and persecutions, however, continued to agitate the Low Countries. It has been estimated that by 1560 no fewer than ten thousand people had fled from the Low Countries to find refuge in England alone. Seizures, tortures, and executions of suspected heretics continued.

The diary of a Brussels citizen supplies a revealing picture of the period. It tells how one afternoon in the Church of Saint Gudula, six children were baptized, the eldest only eleven. Their parents were members of the banned sect of Anabaptists who had been arrested as heretics by order of the bishop, and other citizens served as godparents. After the ceremony, the concluding entry states, ". . . the parents were burned in the marketplace."

More and more events such as these made even devout Catholics sympathize with Protestants and religious reformers.

79 Philistine soldiers, detail of *The Suicide of Saul* (page 123)

The extent of fear is suggested by a letter written in 1561 by Bruegel's friend, the geographer and map publisher Abraham Ortels, or Ortelius, to an acquaintance in Lisbon, Portugal. In it he asked which among the illustrations and ornaments used to decorate maps were now considered suspect by the Inquisition, and which might be safe to use in future.

To add to the tensions in the Low Countries, a financial crisis that had been brewing for some time broke out openly in the great Antwerp Stock Exchange, with severe and widespread economic effects.

Perhaps because of such oppressive conditions, perhaps also because of personal experiences unknown to us, Bruegel by 1561 seemed preoccupied with pictorial symbols of conflict, warfare, and death. He painted violence and hatred in action in hell and in heaven, as well as on man's tormented earth.

His wild painted fantasy called *Mad Meg* in English (*Dulle Griet* in Flemish) shows a gigantic female vixen striding, sword in hand, through hell itself. The demons, monsters of many kinds, flee in terror from her and her army of smaller vixens.

Mad Meg suggests many different meanings. There are folksayings that hell cannot halt a furious and rabid woman. But Bruegel has painted his armored Meg carrying sacks filled with golden loot: coins, cups, jewelry, even a frying pan. She surely symbolizes the plunder perpetrated by mercenary and foreign troops in the wars of the era. Like the allegorical queens in the "Sins" series, she stands for a host of human evils.

In a different vein is Bruegel's *Fall of the Rebel Angels*, showing war-torn heaven at the height of the struggle described in Milton's *Paradise Lost:* on top and victorious, the "good angels," loyal to the Lord; below and being cast down to the pit, the rebellious spirits, under Satan or Lucifer.

The angelic leader, Archangel Michael, is painted as unnaturally tall and slender to symbolize his sanctity. He swings his sword, driving down to hell the new monsters who had till a short time before been blessed angels [80]. In future, because of their impious sedition, they will tempt and torment humankind under the direction of the Prince of Darkness.

This painting is congested, tortured, and strangely medieval in feeling. Its demon monsters symbolize deadly sins. Extreme elongation to suggest sanctity

80 Archangel Michael, detail
of *Fall of the Rebel Angels;*
oil on wood panel, signed
and dated 1562 (Brussels)

is a device Bruegel used several times. It is linked, on the one side, with the Middle Ages, and on the other, reaches toward the intense paintings of El Greco (1541–1614) in Spain.

Again, in *The Suicide of Saul* [81], Bruegel probed the last extremities of a desperate ruler, illustrating a vivid part of the Old Testament (I Samuel 31).

Saul, first king of Israel, has been defeated on Mount Gilboa by the Philistines, shown at right in vast numbers as they complete their slaughter of the Hebrews. Saul's three sons have been slain, and Saul himself sorely wounded by arrows. He orders his armor bearer to kill him so the Philistines will not capture him, but the man refuses. Saul then throws himself on his own sword and dies. Saul here is the crowned figure in armor on the rock at lower left, his throat pierced by his sword. His armor bearer beside him is following the example and is also falling on his sword.

Vast numbers of cavalry and foot soldiers are shown or suggested in the mountain passes at lower right.

81 *Suicide of Saul;* oil on
wood panel, signed and
apparently dated 1562 (Vienna)

Their armor and equipment are, of course, entirely of
the mid-sixteenth century, not of Saul's ancient era.
This is the way the troops of Charles V and later of
Philip II looked as they took part in the sixteenth
century's repeated wars of conquest, dynastic succession,
or religion.

The complex landscape combines elements of the
Low Countries with Alpine cliffs and crags. A populous
city is shown also, though the Bible story does not
require it. A river flows diagonally through the scene,
another Bruegel trademark. Fleeing remnants of
Saul's forces are seeking to escape across this stream
and into the hillside beyond.

This is a tumultuous, tragic picture, marshaling
masses of people in the organized murder called "war."

Bruegel probably completed about half a dozen
paintings in 1562, not one exuberant or even noticeably
optimistic in mood. Quietest, simplest, and most
unusual among them all is the haunting animal "portrait" called *Two Monkeys* [82].

These red-headed captives sit, chained to a ring-bolt
in a window that pierces a thick stone wall. Through
that opening we see, faint and delicate in the mist,
a view of the River Scheldt in the direction of Antwerp
itself. Fragments of food imply that this confinement is
continual.

Many have wondered what Bruegel was seeking
to suggest. Somehow, this haunting picture must
have meaning that does not at first meet the eye.
Bob Claessens, a modern Belgian interpreter of Bruegel,
supplies a suggestion that harmonizes with other
facts. He notes this is a dormer window, a kind commonly found in old fortresses and prisons. Also,
Antwerp is here seen as if from the dormer windows of
Fort Philippe, "where patriots were imprisoned."

Claessens concludes that the monkeys symbolize the
human prisoners, members of the growing "resistance"
movement against King Philip and his agents. As
analogy, Claessens suggests a parallel from World
War II, when Belgium was occupied by the forces of
another foreign dictator, Adolf Hitler. If at that time
"a painter had shown the poor monkeys sadly
imprisoned in the dormer windows of Fort Breedonk,
who could have mistaken that?" Claessens asks.

Claessens also reminds us that it was during 1562, or at latest at the start of 1563, that Bruegel left Antwerp, and also then that his friend Christopher Plantin, the cultured printer and humanitarian, was forced to flee from that city. The *Two Monkeys*, Claessens concludes, served as Bruegel's farewell picture, a symbolic leave-taking from Antwerp.

82   *Two Monkeys*; oil on
wood panel, signed and dated
1562 (Berlin)

XIV Marriage and a New Look at Life

83 Joseph, Mary, and Jesus, detail of *Flight into Egypt*; oil on wood panel (page 129)

The final and most fruitful period of Bruegel's life began in 1563, the year he married and moved from Antwerp to Brussels.

The story most often told of his marriage comes from Van Mander's book, which was published some thirty-five years after Bruegel's death. It is short, colorful—and possibly, though not certainly, true. In Antwerp Bruegel lived with a servant girl and thought seriously of marrying her. However, she was prone to tell lies. He tried to cure her weakness by taking a long stick and cutting a notch in it every time he caught her in a lie, and he warned that if the notches reached the end of the stick, he would not marry her. Before long, according to Van Mander's story, the stick was covered with notches. This marriage did not take place.

Soon afterward, however, Bruegel fell in love with and married Marie Coecke, daughter of his former master. She had been living in Brussels with her widowed mother, Marie Bessemers Coecke, who now asked that Bruegel move to Brussels, leaving Antwerp in order, as Van Mander put it, to get his former mistress "out of sight and out of mind."

That change was important in many ways. Brussels was the court city, seat of the Low Countries government headed by the Regent, Margaret of Parma. It may well have provided new opportunities for Bruegel to find patrons and purchasers for the great paintings that increasingly came from his brush. Meanwhile, he retained his established contacts in Antwerp, not too far away, where he had become well known and esteemed.

Bruegel and his youthful bride took up residence

84 The house at 132 Rue Haute, Brussels, home of Bruegel and his wife; restoration is planned.

in a tall three-story stone-and-brick house with stepped roof line in the so-called Flemish Baroque style. It still stands at 132 Rue Haute (or High Street) in Brussels, above cobblestoned streets [84].

Nearby, in the same district of artisans and workers, stands the Church of Notre Dame de la Chapelle, where the Bruegels were married and where, so far as we know, their two sons were later baptized: Peter the Younger, born in 1564; and, in 1568, Jan (known as Jan the Elder, after he, in turn, had a son christened Jan). In this same church, before the end of 1569, Peter Bruegel himself was buried.

During that nuptial year of 1563, Bruegel painted a charming and tender picture on a theme that may suggest both his departure or escape from the old way of life in Antwerp and his founding of a family in Brussels. It is called *The Flight into Egypt* [85], a small picture less than 15 by 22 inches.

Joseph is seen from the back as he walks down an incline leading the donkey, and Mary is carrying Jesus. Colors are delicate, with the strongest tone the red in Mary's garment. The rocks, cliffs, trees, and broad waterway are typical of Bruegel's Italian and post-Italian landscapes.

A small but significant detail appears on the short tree at right, with a bird in its branches. There, below the bird, is a sort of wayside shrine, from under which an idol is falling. This is a symbol of the downfall of pagan worship after the coming of Jesus and the foundation of Christianity. All in all, this picture betokens change—in place, in way of life, in objects of devotion. The painting, now in London, became the property of the powerful Cardinal Granvelle, intimate adviser to the Regent, Margaret of Parma.

85   Flight into Egypt; oil on wood panel, dated 1563 (London)

Bruegel had a wealthy and influential patron in
Niclaes Jonghelinck, owner of a mansion in Antwerp
and brother of the sculptor Jacques Jonghelinck. Niclaes
became the earliest of the great Bruegel collectors.
At one time he possessed sixteen Bruegel paintings,
among them *The Tower of Babel* of 1563 (see plate 1)
and *The Procession to Calvary* [99], a 1564 subject.

It was for Niclaes that Bruegel painted in 1565 his
masterful series of "Seasons" landscapes. From Brussels,
Bruegel continued also to keep in touch with another
Antwerp friend and admirer, the geographer Abraham
Ortelius, and to supply Jerome Cock with drawings
suitable for engraving.

At this point Bruegel was clearly a mature master,
one who had achieved recognition, respect, and a solid
place in the cultural life of his era. His abilities were
appreciated, for as Van Mander tells in his *Schilderboek*,
"the townsmen of Brussels" gave him a commission
of civic importance. He was to represent in pictures
the digging of the canal that had been completed
between Brussels and Antwerp in the year 1565.
Unfortunately "these pictures were not finished, because
of his death."

It is not strange that Bruegel was chosen for this
assignment, for he had shown brilliantly in many
drawings and paintings his ability to catch the moods
and details of seas, harbors, ships, and the human labors
associated with them. It is doubly unfortunate that the
world lost even such preparatory sketches and designs
as he may have made while still able to work.

Another evidence of esteem is found in the records
of the City Council of Brussels. In the month of January
1569 that body decided, first, to exempt Bruegel's household from the disagreeable duty of providing lodgings
(billets) for Spanish troops then occupying the region;
and, second, to grant him an advance of money for
a commission on a painting. This is added evidence
that Bruegel must have been working, or expecting to
work, less than nine months before his death in
September of that year.

The Bruegel of these final years in Brussels may
indeed have been a man ravaged by physical illness,
disturbed or distressed by the increasing conflicts that
raged in his homeland. Nevertheless, he remained not
only a superlative craftsman with a mature, inquiring

86 Peasant or villager, *From
the Life*; pen and ink drawing,
c. 1566–68 (Rotterdam)

mind, but a personality able to attract and hold superior people as friends, and to reward them with generous gifts of his art and his affections.

His frequent companion during his Antwerp period, and quite possibly also later on in Brussels, was Hans Franckert, a merchant praised by Van Mander as "a noble and worthy man." Franckert originally came from Nuremberg, Germany, and was himself enough of an artist to have been taken into the Antwerp Guild of Saint Luke in 1546, just five years before Bruegel.

Bruegel and Franckert, Van Mander tells, often went out into the countryside, visiting peasant fairs and weddings. They would dress in peasant style, bring wedding presents "like the other guests," and pretend to be family members or friends of the bride or groom.

One last sentence from Van Mander supplies a clue that we can confirm and expand. Bruegel, he wrote, "made many little sketches from life." This has sometimes been translated as "from nature," suggesting they were solely sketches of growing things, landscapes, and so on. There were such, as we have seen in reviewing his Italian and Alpine journeyings. However in his last supreme years, in Antwerp and later Brussels, Bruegel drew, from life, hundreds of his fellow humans.

He drew them when, where, and as he found them, recording their postures, their physical defects and peculiarities, the garments they wore, the tools they carried, and the stamp that their labors had placed on their personalities. On the sketches themselves he would note the colors and fabrics of their garments. Nothing was left to chance. No researcher for a museum or an

87 Seated burgher and legless beggar, *From the Life*; pen and ink drawing, dated c. 1553–55 (London)

88 Studies of three figures, a seated beggar in the center, *From the Life*; pen and ink drawing, c. 1563–64 (Rotterdam)

historical stage production was ever more careful, exact, and scrupulous than Master Bruegel in these *Naer het leven*, or "after the life," sketches that he made for later use. By good fortune, nearly sixty of these masterful records survive, and some of the best are included in this book.

Bruegel's "from the life" drawings include studies of peasants, beggars, burghers, market women, and the like, as well as figures such as the miner, the pilgrim, the horse dealer, and two Jewish rabbis. He observed these people awake, asleep, seated, standing, walking, talking, begging, resting. He shows exactly the appearance of their purses, hats, turbans, cloaks, swords, daggers, axes, hoes, and staffs. Besides this rich human record, there are also drawings of a stag, a buffalo, and a mule.

Scores, perhaps hundreds of other such drawings by Bruegel were destroyed or lost, especially many that may have caricatured or poked fun at people in authority.

In the light of this pursuit of exact appearances, it is easier to understand how he attained the precise, painstaking, and almost loving details that keep his greatest paintings alive and authentic despite the centuries. Bruegel never wearied of watching the world around him—and of preserving it on paper.

This book has already mentioned paintings that Bruegel based on the Bible. During his first three years as a married man in Brussels he painted three more pictures based directly or indirectly on the Bible. They deserve to be mentioned together, for each was a grisaille. A grisaille painting is not a pattern of various colors, but a monochrome—usually varying degrees of gray, from nearly white to black, or of brown.

These three, *The Death of the Virgin, Jesus and the Adulterous Woman,* and *The Resurrection,* reveal much of Bruegel's own sincere reverence for simple goodness and human love.

The imaginative painting of the death of Mary, mother of Jesus, was intimately connected with the artist's personal life. He completed it in 1564 or 1565, using tempera rather than oil paints, on a canvas rather than wood surface. It was intended for his good friend the geographer Abraham Ortelius. About ten years later—five years after Bruegel himself had died—

Ortelius had it engraved by the skilled hand of Philip Galle and then presented prints to various friends of his and Bruegel's as a memorial [89].

The dramatic moment that Bruegel pictures was first described in an old Apocryphal book—meaning one not included in the Bible itself. The story was supposedly told by St. John the Divine, who is shown here, asleep at the fire, far to the left. Meanwhile, as if in a dream or vision, he sees the gathering of about forty disciples, saints, and sages, come to convey the dying Mary to Gethsemane and from there to heaven itself.

The legend mentions several times the miraculous light illuminating Mary. Bruegel shows her shining by her own radiance, rather than by the light of the small taper before her. This powerful contrast of light and shadow anticipates some of the greatest works of Rembrandt in the seventeenth century.

Engraved underneath are twelve lines of Latin poetry appropriate to the picture. In the small box at left appear the Latinized names of "Petri Brugelis" and

89   The Death of the Virgin;
engraved by Philip Galle in
1574, after the grisaille c. 1564
(New York)

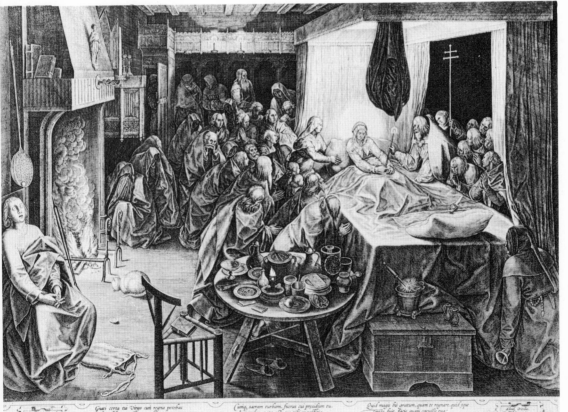

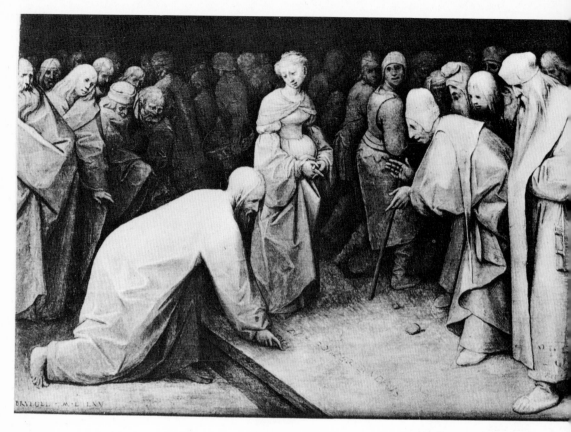

90 Jesus and the Adulterous Woman; grisaille, painted in oil on wood panel, dated 1565 (London)

"Philipp Galleus." The box at right mentions the recipient-donor of this masterpiece, "Abrah. Ortelius."

The chamber in which Mary lies in her canopied bed is a comfortable paneled room in Flemish style, and may resemble one or more rooms of Bruegel's own house in Brussels. The three-legged chair and table in the foreground were common in that era. The beamed ceiling and decorated woodwork are clearly shown. Even the cat dozes comfortably beside the fire.

This sacred drama, full of devotion and tenderness, is played in a setting of solid detail and reality. The imminence of death is emphasized by the muffled mourning figures just right of the fireplace, and by the hooded man in monk's garb at the foot of the bed, holding a bell to toll for departure.

The grisaille—this time in oils rather than tempera—*Jesus and the Adulterous Woman* [90], is dated 1565. Like the previous picture, it, too, became the basis for an engraving after Bruegel's death. And like the other grisaille, its mood is one of tenderness, reconciliation, and—in this case—forgiveness.

This painting "has to be understood as a plea for toleration in the religious strife of Bruegel's time," says Fritz Grossman, an authority on the artist. It depicts an event in the Gospel of John, 8:3–11. The essentials, as adapted from the Bible, follow:

Doctors of the law and other respectable citizens brought a woman to Jesus, saying, "Master, this woman was caught in the very act of adultery. The law of Moses says that such women are to be stoned. What do you say about it?"

This question, the Scripture makes clear, was put as a test or trick in the hope of being able to frame a charge of subversion against Jesus. He, however, bent down and wrote the answer with his finger on the ground: "Let one of you who is free from sin throw the first stone."

After this answer they went away one by one, beginning with the eldest. Jesus, left alone with the woman, asked her, "Where are they? Has no one condemned you?"

"No one, sir," she answered.

Jesus said, "Nor do I. Go, and do not sin again."

Bruegel has pictured the moment when, confronted by Jesus' unanswerable reply, the questioners are turning to leave. A few in the foreground at left and right still stare, fascinated by the implications of the answer, inscribed in the dust of the floor.

Flemish words can be read there on the original: DIE SONDER SONDE IS . . . meaning, "He who is free from sin . . ."

Jesus' face reveals pity and mercy. The sinful woman watches in mingled wonder and hope. Here is the opposite of retribution, hatred, and violence, such as we find in Bruegel's powerful pictures of conflict.

In highly personalized paintings such as these, Bruegel revealed much of his inmost attitudes and his hopes for the world around him.

Space does not permit the presentation of the impressive *Resurrection* grisaille, or the brilliant engraving made from it, probably also by Philip Galle.

This much is certain: a full understanding of Bruegel as painter and thinker must lean heavily on these grisaille paintings. What they lack in color and scope is made up in concentration, candor, and deep inner feeling.

xv The Splendid "Seasons" and Wedding Celebrations

91 Detail of *The Return of the Herd*; oil on wood panel (page 141)

Bruegel painted many of the works that the world has
come to know and love best in the years 1565–66.
It was a wonderful outpouring of genius during those
two years, and also during the next two, 1567–68,
which formed his final period of artistic production.

From 1565 come the five magnificent "Seasons"
landscapes, each depicting the weathers, labors, risks,
and recreations of a particular month or time of year.
Two are reproduced in color in this book: *Hunters in
the Snow, January* or *February;* and *The Corn Harvest,*
probably *August. The Return of the Herd,* very likely
November, is in black and white. *The Stormy* (or
Gloomy) *Day,* probably a *March;* and *Hay-Making,*
either a *June* or *July,* complete this unforgettable group.

These five masterpieces, and perhaps even some
other lost "Seasons" subjects, were painted for
Niclaes Jonghelinck, Bruegel's wealthy patron, and were
intended to decorate a reception room in that rich
merchant's new mansion on Margrave Avenue in
Antwerp. Thus they formed a set, not only in subject
but in intended use. The five that survive are similar in
treatment, harmonious in composition, and rivals in
mastery. Yet each is unique and distinctive.

Each is painted on a wooden panel, about 46 by 63
inches. Each presents in rich detail a fascinating
landscape, seen from above, with laboring humans in
foreground and background, and an abundant vista
with villages, roads, meadows, hills, crags, bodies of
water.

Bruegel's independent approach becomes particularly
clear when we note that Jonghelinck decorated two
other chambers with series or cycles of paintings by
Frans Floris, also called Frans de Vriendt (1517–70), one

of the stellar successes among the Antwerp Romanists or Italianizers. Floris supplied an allegorical series, "The Liberal Arts," for one chamber, and a mythological cycle, "The Labors of Hercules," for another. These panels undoubtedly displayed what he had absorbed during his Italian pilgrimage, when he had faithfully studied Raphael, Michelangelo, and Greco-Roman art relics. Floris, a master in the Antwerp Guild since 1540, was widely regarded as the last word in elegance.

The contrast must have been sharp: the melodrama of the labors of the mythical demigod Hercules in one hall, and the reality of the labors of Bruegel's recognizable Flemish peasants in another!

Hunters in the Snow is perhaps the most magical among pictures of winter, snow-covered lands, and frozen waters (plate III).

In the foreground, at left, three hunters plod through the soft snow, followed by a collection of about a dozen dogs of mingled varieties and sizes. They are passing a line of four bare trees whose bases launch a diagonal across the picture, from lower left toward upper right. A counter-diagonal is formed by the line of the edge of the hill that they are approaching.

An inn is seen at far left, its sign half torn away by the winter wind. In front of its door blazes a fire before which men, a woman, and a child are at work, singeing a freshly slaughtered pig. They bring handfuls of straw to feed the flames. Dark birds perch in the tree branches overhead, and another bird glides toward the right.

Below this hill lies a vista of country fields, roads, and villages swathed in white snow. On frozen ponds skaters glide and stagger. Jagged mountains, also covered with snow, tear into the distant sky. Bruegel has here again combined Alpine crags and Low Countries landscapes in a wonderful world-wide synthesis.

The prevalent green-white hue tells, in color, of cold, silence, and lack of sunshine. It is a magical, muffled world, a world in which nature seems to have suspended activity—yet man labors on, seeks and prepares food, plays, and battles the cold. Despite the white blanketing, the houses and other evidences of man are clear, and somehow welcome.

Bruegel painted the bare branches and their snow coating with enormous and exemplary skill. In total composition, in isolated episodes, and in tiny details, it is

92 The groom, detail of
Wedding Procession; tempera
on wood panel (page 141)

a magnificent pictorial preservation of winter at work
in human lives, and reminds us that Bruegel was
one of the great pioneers in painting snowscapes. This
is not his only painting of snow-carpeted winter scenes.
Two years after this one, in the year 1567, he painted
falling snow in his *Adoration of the Kings in the Snow.*

The Harvesters is sometimes called instead
The Corn Harvest (plate IV). One look shows that the
word corn does not refer to what Americans call
"corn." The grain being harvested is actually wheat,
commonly called *Korn* in the Germanic languages,
including Bruegel's own Flemish.

Here the men and women who have plowed, planted,
and cultivated the grain are harvesting it. Some swing
scythes, others gather and bind to form the tall stacks,
still others have paused for a midday lunch break.
One sleeps, exhausted, under the tall tree just right of
center. The coarse bread they slice and eat was once
grain standing in fields like this.

A general diagonal from lower left to upper right
separates the near scene from the far. Over the yet-
uncut grain we see down into a valley, crossed by roads,
marked by houses and a castle, fenced-in fields for
pasturage, and dotted with people, adult and young,
at work and play. In the distance lie the curved lines
of a lake or sea, which may be derived from Lake
Geneva, as mentioned earlier. At upper right, partially
screened by the tree, is a typical Flemish village church
near which other houses stand.

The peasants are broad, squat, round-faced, not
idealized in the later fashion of a Millet. There may
be a trace of caricature in the drawing, but Bruegel
has not degraded them or belittled their work. One
feels rather that their years of incessant seasonal labors
and drudgeries have shaped their bodies, hands, and
minds.

The detail and exact specifications of this painting
can be realized only by careful study. Yet the minuteness
of its treatment does not diminish the massive effect
of the composition as a whole. Here is the sweat,
the strain, the fatigue, and also—to some extent—the
sense of skill and satisfaction that hard physical labor
brings to workers who must struggle to maintain life. It
is a great record not only of the real world around the
artist, but of the working men and women of that
world. And this, we must recall, was an era when

PLATE I *The Tower of Babel*; oil on wood panel, signed and dated 1563 (Vienna)

PLATE II *Children's Games*; oil on wood panel, signed and dated 1560 (Vienna)

PLATE III   *The Hunters in the Snow, January or February*; oil on wood panel, signed and dated 1565 (Vienna)

PLATE IV *The Harvesters*, or *The Corn Harvest*, probably *August*; oil on wood panel, signed and dated 1565 (New York)

PLATE V *Peasant Wedding*, or *Wedding Banquet*; oil on wood panel, c. 1568 (Vienna)

PLATE VI *Peasant Dance*, or *Kermess*; oil on wood panel, signed but not dated; c. 1568 (Vienna)

PLATE VII   *The Parable of the Blind*; tempera on canvas, signed and dated 1568 (Naples)

PLATE VIII   *Storm at Sea, or Jonah and the Whale*; oil on wood panel, c. 1568 (Vienna)

manual labor hardly seemed a suitable subject for master artists and their wealthy or aristocratic patrons.

The Return of the Herd [93] is an autumnal symphony of rich browns, yellows, dark grays, and other warm tones. Half a dozen "cowboys"—after the Flemish fashion—drive along a herd of perhaps eighteen cattle. Their chief, muffled against the cool air, rides a horse. The rest of the workers are afoot, carrying long poles to use as cattle prods.

Only two human faces appear. The rest are turned from us, and all but two of the cattle are turned away as they walk. A white-and-black cow occupies center foreground. Behind her runs a cowherd with heavy features. Just beyond his head we catch sight of a distant bird trap on the hill.

In the distance are hills planted with vineyards in which peasant workers are laboring. Beyond them, a curved river flows diagonally into the distance. In small but rich detail we see, on its far side, boats, a dock, houses, and other objects, while above them looms a massive and rugged mountain of Alpine cast.

At upper left, on the "near side" of the stream, stands a partly ruined round tower, and beyond it a series of peaks and bluffs overshadowing the river valley at their feet.

The cattle are being driven between leafless trees, and the picture as a whole is framed, left and right, by nearby trees shown in lifelike detail of bark and texture. High in the tree at left perches a dark bird. A rainbow arches faintly over the distant river valley, while dark clouds mass in the sky.

Like the rest of the "Seasons" cycle, this is a triumph of rich and appropriate coloration. Blues blend with browns, gray-greens with off-whites. Each of the human figures is firmly molded, solid, even statuesque. Bruegel here, as so often in his records of everyday labors and amusements, presents faithful and familiar types, not personalized portraits.

Bruegel triumphed in his recording of the unending cycles of tasks and labors through the seasons, yet in drawing and in painting he was no less in tune with the fairs, festivals, recreations, and even the riotous interludes that broke into the labors of his Flemish fellow countrymen.

During 1566–67 in particular he recorded in a series

93 *The Return of the Herd;* oil on wood panel, signed and dated 1565 (Vienna)

of paintings three typical scenes of weddings as celebrated by the peasants of the regions of Brabant and the Campine. One of these, *Wedding Dance in the Open Air*, was painted in 1566; another, called either *Peasant Wedding* or *Wedding Banquet*, was painted in 1567 (plate v). The third, *Wedding Procession* [94], has only recently been identified with some certainty as the work of Peter Bruegel the Elder rather than of one of his sons.

The last is a wide, low landscape dominated by the double lines of the procession. Two groups are walking, each following a bagpiper. Closer to us is the procession of women led by the fat bride, eyes downcast, hands clasped, and wearing a crown upon her head. A pair of young pages walk on either side, like an honor guard, with a dozen or more village women following.

The men's contingent is more numerous. The groom is also crowned; framed between two trees at left, he looks nervous and uncomfortable. His father, wearing an elaborate robe, walks behind him, followed by a scattered but determined collection of peasants and villagers. Using reds, blues, greens, and black, Bruegel has set off their garments richly.

A windmill grinds in the middle distance; houses, barns, a church, and a flock of sheep appear between the trees above the groom's head. A white highlight at

94 *Wedding Procession;* tempera on wood panel, c. 1566–67 (Brussels)

95 Two beggars, *From the Life;* pen and ink drawing, undated (Berlin)

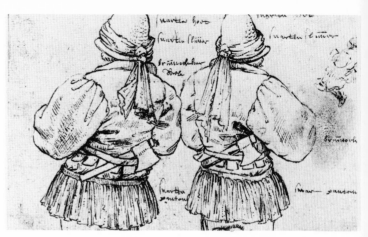

96 Woodcutters, *From the Life*; pen and ink drawing, c. 1565 (Berlin)

the lower-right corner is the skull of a sheep.

This painting, executed in tempera on a wood panel, is unsigned. The skillful placement of the people in the two separate yet interweaving processional lines is one of the arguments for attributing it to Peter Bruegel the Elder.

Peasant Wedding is not signed or dated either, yet is unquestionably Bruegel's work, and one of his very greatest. It was most probably painted in 1566 or 1567. Large figures appear in the foreground. In fact, the largest figure—that of the aproned man holding up the rear of the barn door that doubles as a serving tray— takes up about three-fifths of the total height of the painting.

By bold placement and perspective, Bruegel puts us close to the handsome pourer (at lower left) and to the child, partly submerged under a huge feathered hat, who tastes banquet fare (farther right).

The wedding feast takes place in a barn. The "sit-down guests" around the table number about twenty, the maximum permitted for such peasant celebrations by the decrees of Charles V, which were continued in effect by Philip II. However, at the far end of the barn (upper left) we see party crashers, onlookers, and refreshment sharers crowding into the door.

Two awkward bagpipers stand beside the crude benches, probably the village piper (facing us) and his son, whose puffed cheeks suggest he is now playing. A pair of pipers also led the double procession to church in the previous picture!

The bride is easy to find. Still crowned, she sits smiling, almost stupidly smug, before a blanket hung on the wall. The groom, however, is not next to her.

Three places to her right (our left) he sits, wide-eyed
and busily pushing food into his mouth. Next to him sits
a white-haired man apparently offering him advice—
probably his father.

The parents of the bride are on her left (our right):
first her mother, then her father, wearing a dark hat and
sitting in the armchair of honor. Still farther right is
a hooded man—a monk or friar. Then a bearded man
in rich, dark garb, wearing a sword.

This nonpeasant guest has stimulated various
guesses. Is he a neighboring landlord who has accepted
the invitation of his tenant? Is he some rich relative
from a nearby town? Or is this, as some have surmised,
a self-portrait of Bruegel himself? We recall Van
Mander's report that Bruegel, together with his friend
Franckert, liked to go to peasant weddings and
festivals, pretending to be kinspeople. And this does
look like a quiet, contemplative man, somewhat amused.

Exceptionally large, few, and bold figures make up
the *Peasant Dance,* an undated painting, completed
about 1567 (plate VI). It shows Bruegel's later style
of bigger, more concentrated composition. This is a
Flemish fair holiday, or *Kermess,* with dancing on the
village street outside the inn.

The bagpiper (at left) puffs his cheeks as he sits on
a bench beside the outdoor table. A young man
solicitously looks into his face, offering him a drink of
ale to wet his whistle. Two children, the smaller
probably not over two or three years old, imitate their
dancing elders. We can feel, if not hear, the surge
and rhythm of the music. The dancers, in spite of age
differences, are energetic and exuberant.

At the table behind the bagpiper sit three heavy
drinkers, two of whom have become quarrelsome. Back
of them stand a couple kissing. At the door of the
inn a young man tries to pull out a girl to join him in
dancing. Farther to the right, along the picket fence,
stands a peasant clad in the traditional costume of the
fool, part of the funmaking of a full-fledged *Kermess.*
The village church stands at the far end of the street.

This painting has received much deserved praise.
It is dynamic, simple in structure, and compelling in
effect. Also it illustrates an idea often expressed in
a popular Flemish proverb: "As their elders sing, so pipe
the young folks."

XVI Masterworks from Troubled Times

97 Gentleman, believed to be Hans Franckert, and fortuneteller, detail of *Sermon of Saint John the Baptist*; oil on wood panel (page 157)

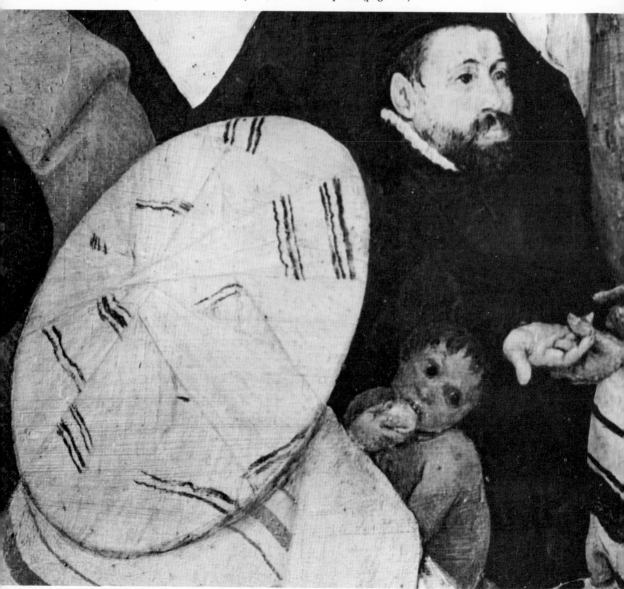

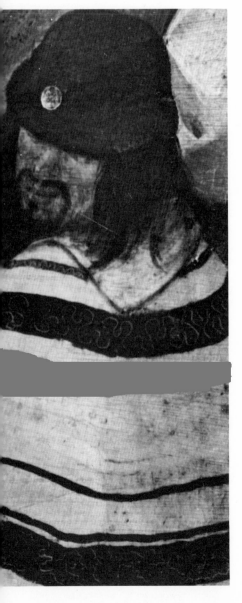

Bruegel's growth in power, scope, and variety is most apparent in paintings completed during his final five years of artistic life. Yet in his drawings, also, he attained new heights of human insight and importance. Probably his most fascinating single drawing was completed in one of the years from 1565–68: *The Artist and the Connoisseur*, sometimes called also *Painter and Patron*, or *Artist and Amateur*, or even *Self-Portrait with a Patron* (page 39).

This was without doubt one of the Bruegel works most sought after and imitated in his lifetime, since four copies of it are known, and experts are divided as to whether one or two of them were executed by Bruegel himself.

One of the four copies was found with a piece of paper attached stating that this was a portrait of Jerome Bosch. If true, it would be amazing. The evidence, however, does not support such a connection. Yet this tense, tormented face, with its tight-pressed lips and penetrating gaze, does appear to be a faithful and highly personal portrait, not just an imaginative generalization.

Many art historians believe this is actually Bruegel's self-portrait, drawn—as usual in such cases—with the help of several mirrors. Whether or not it is, Bruegel has depicted a revealing, ironical, and even satirical little drama—exposing the inevitable clash between the creative artist and the patron or public he must please in order to live.

The artist stands, brush in hand before his easel, unkempt, unhappy, intent only on the effort to complete his work. Peering fatuously over his shoulder from a smug position of critical evaluation is the connoisseur,

or patron. His mouth is open ever so slightly as he
hesitates over some remark. His long nose seems
to sniff at the work and his narrowed eyes peer out
through sixteenth century spectacles.

The sterile onlooker clearly has power over the dour
artist. This is emphasized by a significant but ambiguous gesture: the patron's hand is at the mouth
of a fat purse hanging from his belt. Is he reaching in
so as to make the artist an offer of money for the
work? Or is he withdrawing his hand, empty?

The picture implies a conflict and poses a question,
or a series of questions. Here is a rare personal comment
by the artist on his own work and position in the
world. This drawing, indeed, could be taken as a
symbol of the contrasting situations of the creator and
the patron in each and every art.

The painter is clearly neither relaxed nor comfortable.
Posture, facial expression, tangled hair and neglected
beard, curved back and projected neck, cramped
stance of the hand that clutches the brush—all these
have seemed to some observers to point in one significant
and tragic direction. This artist must be a victim of
multiple arthritis, in which the joints become inflamed,
enlarged, and rigid.

The art historian Gotthard Jedlicka has argued
energetically that this not only is a self-portrait but
shows Bruegel in an advanced stage of arthritis. Experi-
menting with arthritics, Jedlicka found that to hold a
brush, they, too, were forced to use index and middle
fingers with the thumb merely in an assisting role,
as the painter appears to do here. The handle of the
brush in the picture, furthermore, is not round. It has a
flat, rectangular cross-section. This too is offered as
evidence that the artist was forced to use special tools in
order to continue his work.

Such an interpretation of the drawing was, in fact,
presented in August 1953 at an international meeting of
medical specialists in rheumatic ailments held in
Switzerland. A Belgian writer on Bruegel, Bob Claessens,
notes: "The face itself reveals, in its stretched cheeks
and tight-pressed mouth, bitterness and resignation—
fruits of long suffering, such as doctors generally
find in the chronic forms of multiple arthritis." He
suggests that the neglected hair and untrimmed beard
are "silent witnesses of the inability . . . to raise his

98 Peasant woman, *From the Life;* pen and ink drawing, c. 1565 (Berlin)

arms and so to give attention to his hairdress."

Here again we have only meager evidence. If during his last years Bruegel, like the French impressionist Renoir, was virtually a cripple, this would help to explain, says Claessens, "why he lived in such retirement toward the end of his life, why he died so unexpectedly, why his works present us with so many paralytics and disabled people, and why we have no painting of his dated 1569, even though he did not die until the end of that year."

Symptoms so severe as those Jedlicka finds in this drawing suggest that the victim must have been at least forty-five years old at the time. Assuming that the drawing was made in 1565, this leads Jedlicka to suppose that Bruegel was born in 1520 rather than in the period 1525–30 generally assigned to his birth.

During the final productive years of Bruegel's career in art, tensions between the Low Countries and the Spanish rule erupted into open conflicts. They are

99 *The Procession to Calvary,*
or *The Carrying of the Cross;*
oil on wood panel, signed
and dated 1564 (Vienna)

reflected in Bruegel's dark and bitter masterworks of the
period between 1565–68. Eight are related more or
less unmistakably to events of that era, even though
outwardly most of them are based on subjects taken
from the New Testament.

The earliest of this group is *The Procession to
Calvary*, also called *The Carrying of the Cross* [99–101].
Largest of all Bruegel's paintings, it fills nearly 49 by 67
inches of wood paneling, and portrays the sun-drenched
and dreadful pageant of a public execution, carried
out amidst purely Flemish conditions and costumes.

Red-coated soldiers accompany a procession of
condemned prisoners in the middle distance. They move
through a crowd of onlookers toward the execution
site, a hill of medium size at upper right. On its slopes
grow a gruesome crop of gallows, tall wheels, and
distant crosses erected for crucifixion, the terrible Roman
form of capital punishment.

One must search the crowded scene before discover-
ing, almost at the exact center, but small and obscure

in emphasis, the figure of Jesus, fallen under the weight
of the cross. To the right, farther along in the
procession, a cart carries the two thieves, accompanied
by a priest—of the Roman Catholic Church!

This then is an execution conducted by the forces
of Authority: the red-coated Spanish troops plus a
Church representative. In name only is it a picture of a
place called Judea under Roman rule. It is, in fact,
the Low Countries under Spanish rule. And, as if to
show that most people are unaware or don't care,
Bruegel has filled the panel with hundreds of humans
engaged in manifold everyday actions and activities.
The business, the encounters, the petty crimes, and the
commotions of ordinary existence are taking place
quite as usual while Jesus of Nazareth staggers toward
the hill where "justice" is to be carried out.

In the foreground, and as if cut off by size and style
of painting from the remainder of the picture, we
see the mourners: Mary, mother of Jesus, is supported
by Saint John the Evangelist; and the other two Marys,

100   Children playing, detail of
The Procession to Calvary

in sixteenth century dress, kneel facing her, and pray.
This traditional group appears neither to see, nor to be
seen by, the antlike crowd beyond.

A study of the complex detail in this picture would
require many pages. It is a composition of enduring
fascination and revelation. Through skillful coloring
as well as drawing its mood is set and underscored. A
fresh, natural green dominates at the left, from which
the procession has come. But on the ghastly hill of
execution all is barren, as if frozen by death. The sky too
reflects this contrast: clear and tender at left, gloomy
and stormy at right above the gibbets.

Symbols of life and growth are at left; of destruction

101 The Virgin Mary; also
Jesus and the crowd in the
background, detail of *The
Procession to Calvary*
(page 150)

and death at right. The procession moves from life toward this death on the crest of the fatal site. Several flying carrion birds underscore the mood of menace, and one perches patiently on a tall wheel at right foreground.

At the foot of the pole that supports this wheel, almost at the right margin of the picture, two men stand watching the scene. One of them, his sad, thoughtful bearded face seen in profile, has been identified as Bruegel himself by an art critic named Auner. This figure's hands are clasped as if in prayer, but his eyes do not turn away. His companion, too, has a notably sad and tragic face.

The vivid, dramatic stories of the Bible have provided
analogies and symbols for the struggles of many people
during past centuries. The story of the escape of the
Children of Israel from bondage to the Egyptians in the
time of the Pharaohs, for example, meant more to
exploited slaves in the South during the first half of
the nineteenth century than just a series of incidents
dating back several millennia. It was the living symbol
of a dream and a goal: *Let my people go!*

Bruegel, too, clearly a keen and critical reader of the
Bible, found in the Scriptures a series of apt, bold, and
inspired illustrations of the concerns and griefs
of his own time and place.

Here is his interpretation of the events from Luke
2:1–5, *The Numbering of the People at Bethlehem* [102],
a painting of 1566. The Biblical story declares that
the Roman Emperor, Augustus, had decreed "that all
the world should be taxed." For this purpose every man
was to go back to his native town and register—a
census, in other words, in which the population sought
out the census-takers.

Joseph, a carpenter working in Nazareth, returned
to Bethlehem, the traditional "city of David" in Judea,
with his betrothed, Mary. She was pregnant, and
gave birth to her first child, a son, during their very
first night in Bethlehem.

Bruegel makes Bethlehem a winter-bound Flemish
village, where taxation was all too familiar, though
the proceeds flowed to King Philip II of Spain rather
than to the Emperor Augustus in Rome. The registration
takes place here at the village inn (lower left). A small
crowd stands outside the window, within which sits
the clerk with his telltale lists. Next to him stands
the fur-clad tax collector, his left hand extended to
receive coins from the registrants before they are free
to leave.

On the snow-covered roads and frozen ponds people
come and go, labor, amuse themselves, skate, bear
burdens. Only after searching does one find the principal
characters of the sacred history. In the foreground,
somewhat right of center, a bent Joseph leads the mule
bearing Mary, hooded and blanketed.

No radiance, no glory, no glamor envelopes these
humble, hard-pressed human travelers. They have
arrived, unheralded and ungreeted, at an inn where no
room awaits them. A cow, wandering at large in the

*102   The Numbering of the
People at Bethlehem;* oil on
wood panel, signed and dated
1566 (Brussels)

snowy village square, does not turn aside to let them
pass. The path before them is blocked by great barrels
on wheels, probably containing beer. Chickens pick
at the snowy ground. A pig is being slaughtered
(at lower left), further evidence that this is indeed
the land of the Flemings, not Judea, land of the Jews,
to whom pork is forbidden!

People huddle about a fire to keep warm, close to a
building of typical Low Countries brick construction
(near the painting's center). Children, dogs, workers,
and wagons are scattered about in confusion. It is
the ordinary, everyday routine of such a village at about
sundown on a bitterly cold day. In one bold, clear
leap Bruegel has moved from the Gospel story into his
own Brabantine countryside. Bethlehem has become,
in fact, a part of the region around Brussels!

Another great painting of 1566, *The Sermon of*

Saint John the Baptist [104], also gives a Flemish setting to a Scriptural theme. The prophet-preacher stands in the distance, pointing with his left arm at one man in the crowd of listeners—Jesus, standing not far away, in a light garment, his arms folded before him.

These are Biblical figures, but all the rest are wholly and solely sixteenth century Flemings. It is almost a "news illustration" of the way many Protestant spokesmen, mainly Calvinists, were at that time carrying their messages to the people. They preached in the fields, outside the town, in defiance of the drastic decrees against such heresies.

Such outdoor preaching was especially prevalent in 1566. It was said that these eloquent and emphatic "preachers in the green" seemed to spring up from all sides. In a great Brussels print collection today is an engraving by Franz Hogenberg called *Calvinist Preaching in the Fields*. Its date, too, is 1566.

In his *Revolt of the Netherlands*, Friedrich von Schiller, the famous German poet, dramatist, and historian, said, "A great many were attracted by this preaching . . . in which the Pope, the Fathers of the Council of Trent, and other dogmas of the ruling Church were abused in a comical way." In fact, "an applause, like that in a theater, rewarded the preacher who most outdid the others."

Bruegel's painting shows a varied audience of townspeople, workers, peasants, monks, and even gypsies. One listener seems to belong to the upper class—in center foreground, the bearded man in dark suit and hat, his face somewhat turned toward us, his palm being read by a gypsy [97]. This gentleman's face is so distinctive that it seems certain to be an actual portrait. Some have speculated that Bruegel may here have shown his good friend Hans Franckert.

This is one of Bruegel's richest paintings in varieties of types and personalities. Here is the ripe fruit of his many faithful studies "from the life" made in the streets and byways of Antwerp, Brussels, and elsewhere.

The year 1566 was a bloody turning point in Low Countries history. It is still often referred to as "the year of wonders" because of its extraordinary and unprecedented events. The nobles of the Low Countries, determined to increase their influence against the rigid rule of Philip II of Spain, had formed working alliances

103 Members of the crowd (top) and Saint John the Baptist (right), details of Sermon of Saint John the Baptist

104 Sermon of Saint John the Baptist—Jesus is to the right of Saint John; oil on wood panel, signed and dated 1566 (Budapest)

with the growing Calvinist movement, especially in the regions of Antwerp, Brussels, and the South.

Meanwhile, Protestant craftsmen, driven from the Low Countries by the persecutions of the Inquisition there, had found refuge in large numbers in England. Their products now began to cut into the trade of their homeland.

By this time the Netherlands nobles felt forced to resist the Inquisition if they could. A petition was drawn up and signed by two thousand nobles, officers of local police and armed forces, and church officials. The signers swore to defend their country's traditional rights, to expel the Inquisition, and (at the same time!) to stay loyal to their monarch, Philip II of Spain. This historic document came to be called the "Compromise of the Nobles." Actually, for its time, it seemed quite uncompromising!

Early in April 1566 three hundred noble officers, marching solemnly two by two, bore this compromise to the Brussels palace of Margaret of Parma. There

105 Listener in prayer, detail of *Sermon of Saint John the Baptist* (page 157)

they presented it to her, in an unheard-of gesture of
resistance. Margaret, knowing that the compromise also
had the support of the Council of State and the Privy
Council of the Low Countries, was alarmed, and showed
her fears. Then, as a famous story tells, a courtier
near her said reassuringly, "Fear nothing, madam; they
are only beggars."

A few days later a banquet was held by these
petitioning nobles. The count who had placed the
document in the Regent's hand now distributed beggars'
bowls and pouches to the guests. A glass was raised.
A toast rang out: "Long live the Beggars!" A roar
of approval resounded.

The new slogan took root rapidly. *Les Gueux*—the
Beggars—became the sign and symbol of the resisting
nobles and their supporters, who hoped now that
they were on the way to establishing a republic headed by
their aristocratic group. They dressed in beggars' gray
and even grew beards and mustaches of typically
beggarly shapes.

Townspeople too joined this resistance movement.
They flaunted badges bearing a picture of King
Philip II, of a beggar's pouch, and of two hands clasped.
The attached slogan suggested, "We're loyal to the
king—until we're forced to go begging."

A nasty economic and industrial crisis underlay the
situation. The harvest had been bad. Inflation, already
troublesome in Western Europe, was intensified. Food
prices shot upward. The unemployed and destitute
became desperate and demanded changes.

In August of 1566 this social tinder burst into flame.
In the regions of Armentières and Hondeschoote
bands of industrial workers and the jobless, in part
incited by provocateurs and agents working for King
Philip, broke into churches, smashed statues, and
slashed pictures.

Thus began the "iconoclastic"—or image-smashing
—outbreaks. Spreading like wildfire from town to
town, by September they had reached Leeuwarden, in
the far northern Low Countries. Then they died out.
The purpose of the great majority of the "iconoclasts"
had not been plunder. Frustrated and bitter, they had
thought they were destroying the "idolatry of Rome"
and purifying their houses of worship. Many of
them had turned over precious church ornaments to
local authorities, who generally took no action against

the participants in the outbreak.

But the Spanish rule moved toward drastic reprisals.
Margaret of Parma imported German troops to crush
this resistance and expelled all foreign pastors from
the Low Countries. From Spain, Philip II sent as avenger
his most formidable and merciless military leader, the
Duke of Alva.

Alva assembled a force of some nine thousand troops
at Milan, and marched them north via Savoy, Franche-
Comté, and Lorraine. They entered Brussels in August
1567, just a year after the start of the "iconoclastic"
outbreaks. Alva came with unlimited authority.
Philip II had declared, "I am determined to destroy the
country completely if I can in no other way rule it as I
wish." Mercenaries from German and Walloon sources
swelled the Duke's forces to sixty thousand. The
German *Reitres* wore a blue-steel armor, known as the
black harness, while the Spanish and Walloons were
clad in red cuirasses.

Thus began a reign of blood and terror. The more
farsighted among the resisters in the Low Countries
had fled to England or Germany—as many as a hundred
thousand may have escaped even before Alva occupied
Brussels. Now he sealed off every possible exit and
the blood of his victims flowed. He executed leading
nobles, destroyed their castles and citadels, legally
murdered thousands of citizens of all classes and kinds.

The final outcome, however, was not to be the
complete crushing of Low Countries resistance. The
northern provinces, after epic difficulties and discourage-
ment, finally established their independence from the
Spanish crown. (They achieved this nearly two centuries
before the American colonists won independence from
King George III of Britain and established the United
States.)

In 1568, Bruegel, still working in a Brussels ruled
by the Duke of Alva, painted one of his most fascinating
and enigmatic pictures, called either *The Beggars* or
The Cripples [106]. It hangs in the great Louvre of
Paris—a small work that poses many questions.

Here five horrible mutilated figures hobble in
contrasting positions on the ground. All but one wear
foxtails. In the right background a woman walks away.
She carries the empty bowl from which she has
apparently served them a few crumbs.

Scholars have speculated widely on the meaning of

106 The Beggars, or *The Cripples;* oil on wood panel, signed and dated 1568 (Paris)

this painting. A most plausible suggestion is that these figures symbolize the noble Beggars known in Bruegel's day as *Les Gueux,* or *Gueuse.* True, by 1568 the power of that movement had been drowned in blood by the Duke of Alva and his armies so far as the Brussels-Antwerp region was concerned. Yet to the north, in the area now the Netherlands, the defiant Beggars continued to resist Philip's forces by sea and land. In fact, it has been pointed out that by 1568 guerrilla forces of the Beggars movement were ready to go into action against Alva.

If these are beggars of that sort, then what could be the meaning of the woman who walks away? Most probably she would represent Margaret of Parma, Regent for Philip II until just after the arrival of Alva. She had made some concessions to the Beggars', or nobles', party. Then, after Alva arrived like an avenging demon, she had resigned her office and left the Low Countries altogether. She had, as it were, abandoned the Beggars.

As for the foxtails and the coarse cloth these beggars wear, they relate to the chosen costumes of the movement. The foxtails were associated also with the Beggars' support of a writer named Felix Renard (the French word for "fox") who had been active in opposing Cardinal Granvelle, the private adviser to Philip II and Margaret of Parma until shortly before.

In any case, these five raw, misshapen beings represent, or even satirize, a variety of different social classes in 1568. The right-hand cripple, his back toward us, wears a bishop's miter of paper, and thus stands for the Church. The next figure, his mouth agape in a shout or scream, wears the shako of a soldier and represents the military. Next, facing left, is a peasant figure. Behind him, his back to us, is the cloaked townsman or scholar. Finally, and farthest left, is the brutal symbol of royalty, his mock crown falling over his eyes as if to blind them.

No wonder that a perceptive writer, R. L. Delevoy, has said, "This powerful yet delicately executed work records with unflinching objectivity the misery of the human lot at its most abject."

Mass violence and its resulting agonies are recorded in Bruegel's powerful painting *The Massacre of the Innocents* [107]. Executed in oils on a wooden panel, it is undated. It is often supposed to date from as early as 1565 or '66, but the present authors incline to the view that it was not completed until late '67 or even '68, when the Alva terror was rampant in the Low Countries.

Two versions survive, both showing signs of damage during the centuries. One hangs in the royal palace of Hampton Court, England. The other is in the great Art Historical Museum of Vienna. The latter is the one illustrated, for it depicts most clearly the action that Bruegel intended. The Hampton Court painting, though it contains Bruegel's characteristic brushwork and figure-modeling, was altered by later retouchers, who deliberately weakened the horror of some of the events in the massacre of infant children.

The snow-covered square of a Flemish village is invaded by a company of ruthless soldiers, quite obviously Spanish. Nevertheless, they are supposed to be Roman troops, acting on orders of King Herod who, according to Matthew 2:16, "gave orders for the massacre of all children in Bethlehem and its neighborhood, of the age of two years or less."

Once again, Palestine in the days of the infancy of Jesus is represented by Bruegel's own Low Countries, disfigured by the blood of atrocities. Foot soldiers break down doors, seizing and slaughtering innocent children. Fathers and mothers on their knees beg for mercy, but the soldiers pay no attention: they have their

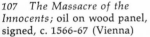

107   The Massacre of the Innocents; oil on wood panel, signed, c. 1566-67 (Vienna)

orders and they are just "doing their duty."

Scattered about the square are a dozen or more heartrending incidents. Parents flee, soldiers pursue. Children are carried off and put to the sword. These are the storm troopers of the Duke of Alva and of Philip II, obeying the royal edicts.

Some of the child-killing soldiers wear red cuirasses, similar to those of the soldiers in the *Carrying of the Cross*, and thus they are linked to the Spanish soldiery of the day. In the background stands a reserve troop of cavalry, wearing black cuirasses like those of the period's German *Reitres*. Their commander, an old man with a long beard, wears dark garments. In 1568 Alva himself was nearly sixty, but hard, dried-out, and older-looking, his long face elongated further by his pointed beard.

At the right a group of eight or nine peasants desperately but vainly implore mercy from a mounted figure who is either the herald or the deputy of the royal authority that has ordered the massacre: his gesture suggests both a shrug and a refusal. To make the analogy entirely clear, his vest, embroidered in gold, incorporates the design of the two-headed eagle, emblem of the royal House of Hapsburg whose principal figure at the time was King Philip II of Spain!

Thus the Biblical massacre of the innocents is wholly transformed into an organized atrocity perpetrated in the Low Countries during Bruegel's own era. It was indeed an age of blood and fears, and it left an indelible mark on those sensitive spirits who observed and survived it. Beside the large numbers who fled the Low Countries altogether, an estimated six to eighteen thousand people were summarily executed. This painting of Bruegel's must be one of the age's records of human reactions to terror and cruelty.

How did such a bold picture survive? It may have been protected by its Biblical title and source, but more likely it remained hidden during the worst years of the Alva overlordship. The softening of the Hampton Court version was deliberate, very likely to avoid offense to the powerful. Savage soldiers are seizing and carrying off, not innocent children, but a goose, a calf, a bag of grain, and other edibles; in short, they are plundering—not taking babies to kill! There is no reasonable doubt, however, that what Bruegel created in the first place was the slaughter of innocent infants, not the stealing of provisions for a feast of the mercenaries.

If there were any doubt, it would be dispelled by the comment made by Van Mander in his early sketch of the life and achievement of Bruegel. He singled out this picture in particular, as having "much to see that is done true to life." He mentions "a whole family begging for the life of a peasant child, whom a murderous soldier has seized in order to kill." Especially real, he noted, were the mother's "grief and swooning."

No wonder later scholars have paid tribute to the intensity of this painting. Though artistically it is not one of Bruegel's greatest, it is one of his most fiery in effect. Constant van de Wall, calling attention to the way the Spanish soldiers "represent the Roman oppressors" of the Biblical period, declared that Bruegel's paintings "had a burning actuality for their time," even though in our time "scholars have not yet explained all the events and relationships" he depicted.

These are by no means all the Bruegel paintings that seem to reflect the stresses, struggles, and griefs of his era. Only a work far larger than this could do justice to them all. Enough has been shown, however, to provide understanding for Bruegel's dying request to his wife. According to Van Mander, he told her to destroy various pictures that were "too biting and too sharp." Clearly this referred not only to written captions but also to the satirical and caricaturing pictorial content.

Bruegel's reason for this request, according to Van Mander, was "remorse or fear that the most unpleasant consequences might grow out of them." The great painter, beyond doubt, wanted to protect his wife and infant sons from such "unpleasant consequences"— meaning the prosecutions or persecutions of the summary courts set up by the Duke of Alva, then the dictator of the region. Unfortunately, this deprived the world of drawings and probably of paintings that might have shown Bruegel as a social and political satirist of the rank of Daumier and Goya.

Much as the loss may be regretted, the circumstances were such that we must be grateful for the magnificent works that Marie Bruegel and other owners did not feel forced to burn, for Peter Bruegel the Elder was not an artist who stood aside from the great issues of his day.

XVII *Final Triumphs*

108 Fame, detail of *The Triumph of Time*, engraving (page 174)

Bruegel steeped himself in the daily concerns of his
fellow countrymen. Through his art he showed how they
worked and rested, how they stood and walked, the
tools they used, and the amusements they preferred.
He also must have relished the ways they talked, for no
other great artist has been more fascinated by folksayings and popular proverbs.

This concentration continued into his final creative
year of 1568. Here is a simple yet intriguing illustration
whose meaning unfolds in full only when it is linked
with the appropriate popular saying. It is called
sometimes *The Proverb of the Bird's Nest*, sometimes
The Peasant and the Birdnester [109], which means a
nest-stealer.

In a pleasant flat Flemish countryside, free from all
Alpine peaks and even lacking a background river
or sea, a peasant walks toward us, smiling slightly,
though he is just about to step into the water at his
feet. He points, meanwhile, over his shoulder at a
sturdy tree, just climbed by a boy who is losing his hat
while reaching with his left hand to rob the bird's nest.

A great Bruegel student, G. H. de Loo, discovered,
early in this century, the Low Countries proverb behind
this action. Like so many, it is in rhyme. Very freely
translated, it says:

> *The one who knows the nest's location,*
> *Can say that he has known.*
> *The one who steals the nest, however,*
> *Has it for his own.*

The peasant who points as he walks is the knower.
The tree-climbing thief, on the other hand, is about
to become the possessor.

Nest-stealing also appeared in a different sense as a

Om dat de Werelt is soe ongetru
Daer om gha ic in den ru

109 The Proverb of the Bird's Nest, or The Peasant and the Birdnester; oil on wood panel, signed and dated 1568 (Vienna)

symbol for overconfidence and stubborn following of one's own ideas or impulses. Sebastian Brant (1457–1521), author of *The Ship of Fools*, which influenced both Jerome Bosch and Bruegel, put it this way:

> *Who thinks his own ideas are sound*
> *And climbs to steal a nest he's found*
> *Will often fall down to the ground.*

The nest thief here appears to be in some danger of doing just that.

The simplicity and concentration of this illustrated instance of folk wisdom contrasts strikingly with the complexity of Bruegel's *Netherlands Proverbs*, painted only nine years earlier, in 1559 (see pages 118 f.).

Another "proverbial" painting leaves no possible doubt as to what saying is represented, for Bruegel himself lettered the phrase at the bottom of this circular picture:

> *Om dat de werelt is soe angetru,*
> *Darr am gha ic en den ru . . .*
> [*The world, I find, is so untrue*
> *Therefore I mourn as I pass through.*]

110 The Misanthrope; tempera on canvas, signed and dated 1568 (Naples)

The Misanthrope [110] is the usual name for this haunting work, bearing Bruegel's signature and the date 1568. It was painted in tempera on canvas, not on a wood panel.

The central character is an old man clad as a monk or hermit; despite his garb, it is doubtful that he is intended to seem truly pious or virtuous. On the far horizon appear the flames and smoke of a distant burning city under siege. This has been called an effort "to signify the state of Flanders under the hard rule of Spain."

Yet the old man has come through all this with a fat purse. He turns his back on the struggle in the world, but he has not given up worldly wealth. For this reason, the picture is sometimes called by such names as *The False Hermit* or *The Hypocrite*.

This makes all the more ironical what is happening to that filled purse, unknown to the old recluse. It is being cut off, stolen from him, by a horrible imp enclosed partly in a crystal globe. This ragged, beggar-like, popeyed demon represents the false world. The crystal globe surmounted with a crucifix is the emblem of worldly power, the orb carried by kings in the hand opposite that which bears the scepter. Here, however, the world-symbol is transparent, revealing the evil within.

Thus we remain uncertain, as so often in reading the meanings of Bruegel. Is this intended to show a situation that serves the old hypocrite right? Or is this simply evidence that the old man, even while he seeks to escape the faithlessness of the world, remains the victim of its fraud, showing that there is really no way out, not even through a hermitlike effort to be alone?

In either case, he is doubly defeated. He is moving from disappointment to added bitternesses. The path ahead of his feet is strewn with sharp thorns or nails. He will be denied even such comforts as his purse could provide. And that insane puppetlike demon of the world will merely mock.

Yet between the embittered old man and the far-off signs of battle lies a peaceful pastoral scene where white and black sheep graze, tended by a pensive shepherd leaning on his staff. In this Low Countries landscape a windmill stands, grinding grain or pumping water from the level ground.

The world of men, the painting suggests, is deceptive and topsy-turvy. However, regarding nonhuman nature, Bruegel seems to anticipate the twentieth century American poet Robinson Jeffers, who wrote, "the world's well-made though."

The simplicity and central unity of this circular composition are striking, as are its use of color and the technique of its painting.

Certainly one of the two or three greatest of all Bruegel works, and possibly one of the ten or twelve finest achievements in all European art is the broad canvas, measuring nearly 61 inches wide by 34 inches deep, known as *The Parable of the Blind* (plate VII).

Had only this survived from Bruegel, he would merit inclusion among the greatest masters of the sixteenth century and would take his place with Rembrandt, Bosch, Rubens, and Van Eyck among the giants of Flemish-Dutch art.

Here again Bruegel has gone to the parables of the Bible for inspiration. The theme is found in Matthew, 15:14. The disciples have just told Jesus that sanctimonious people "are much offended by what you have been saying." He replies, in part, "Leave them alone, they are blind guides, and if one blind man guides another, they will both fall into the ditch."

Other Flemish artworks on the same theme are known. Jerome Bosch made one showing two blind men, as implied in the Biblical quotation. Bruegel himself made an earlier drawing, also with two blind men, and Cornelis Metsys, 1512–79, painted four in a fatal follow-the-leader line.

In showing six men Bruegel was not seeking to outnumber the earlier versions. Rather he was realizing a particularly bold plan of composition. The line of the blind here moves from safety to disaster in a great diagonal progress, or regress, upper left to lower right.

A close kinship exists between this masterpiece and *The Misanthrope*. Both are painted in tempera on canvas rather than on wood, and the painting techniques and choices of color are similar. There is good reason to believe that they were done one after the other.

Note the contrast between the placid, sunny, genuine rural scene around the six men, and the terror toward which they move, surrounded by the darkness that is always with them. At the far right the leader, lying helpless on his back in the ditch, and his immediate follower, wearing the white hat, have already fallen. Then there is a gap, bridged only by the staff, and the last four are seen, each one moving forward more rapidly and insecurely than the one behind him.

R. L. Delevoy, the art historian, has called this the first picture that succeeded in analyzing movement in both space and time. As we look from left to right we see not only the different places or spaces that the blind men occupy at this single instant; we see also, in effect, how each one will be moving a moment, two moments, or three moments later. With only one fallen leader and a single follower, such a sequence in time could not have been suggested.

This analysis of motion almost anticipates the much later invention of the motion picture, and the stroboscopic light which allows successive stages in a motion to be shown on a single piece of film. Joris Ivens, the Dutch motion-picture maker, once declared, "If Bruegel were alive today, he would be a film director."

There are others who believe this picture shows Bruegel to have been a great medical illustrator. In the

late 1890's two physicians, Jean Martin Charcot and
Paul Richer, wrote a work on deformities and ailments
as depicted in art. They noted how accurately Bruegel had
painted the blind men, with eyes upturned rather
than staring forward. Each of the five whose faces are
visible shows a different and identifiable cause of
blindness. For example, the third man from the left
suffers from atrophy of the eyeball. The man just ahead
of him reveals leucoma. The accuracy of this picture
has been praised by specialists on eye ailments. Yet it
was painted in the sixteenth century when medical
knowledge of such ailments was scanty and inaccurate.

Equally noteworthy is the fidelity of the lovely
landscape. There is no doubt where Bruegel stood when
he painted this scene, church and all. He was at the little
village of Pede Sainte Anne near Brussels. Both the
church that appears in the background and the residential
building at the far left are still standing [111]. The
latter, beautifully reconstructed and furnished today,
is still known in the neighborhood as *t' Kasteeltje*,
meaning "the little castle." Its owner, Emmanuel Rycx,
summarizes the relationship of Peter Bruegel to the
major events of his time: "Resistance was the heart of
his paintings"—meaning resistance to the repression
imposed on his land. And regarding Bruegel's attitude
toward the people of the countryside: "Bruegel loved
poor people."

The tower of the old church of Pede Sainte Anne
still looks, stone for stone, just about as it did four
centuries ago when Bruegel faithfully included it in

111 Two views of the church
of the village of Pede Sainte
Anne, near Brussels, which
appears in *The Parable of the
Blind*, painted in 1568 (plate VI

the background of this most magnificent and touching
among all of his paintings. And not far away one
can still find the ditch into which the poor misled blind
men were falling!

It is inaccurate to deal with Bruegel only from the
point of view of the solid earth, even the Brabantine
earth around Brussels. Throughout his creative life he
was a persistent and extraordinary artist of the sea,
a recorder of water in all its aspects and moods.

Wildest and most wonderful of his seascapes, and
very likely the most magnificent sea concept in the
history of painting, is the unsigned, undated work,
about 27½ by 38 inches, called *The Storm at Sea*,
or more rarely, *Jonah and the Whale* (plate VIII). Some
critics consider it an unfinished work. Others hold that
Bruegel took it as far as he intended, and that what
seems unfinished was in fact intentional, bold innovation
—in directions that anticipate the much later style of
"expressionism" in painting.

The sea is tremendous, menacing, overwhelmingly
high, with red-brown, sharply peaked waves under a
brown, lowering storm sky. Yet on the horizon off to the
left some light breaks through, silhouetting a church
tower in a distant city.

On the surface of the surging billows several sailing
vessels, hard pressed, are fleeing toward the left. The
ship farthest left appears to have released oil in an effort
to smooth the troubled waters, for following that
ship's stern like a wake is a great triangular patch of
green, contrasting sharply with the bitter brown.

A vessel near the center is closely followed by an
enormous whale whose wide-open jaws, revealing a vast
pink interior, are about to close on a barrel which has
been cast astern by that second ship. Apparently, in an
effort to escape, the crew of that vessel have followed
some old sea lore: if a whale can be induced to pause and
play with the barrel, it will forget the pursuit for a
while, or even forego it entirely.

But there is more than one whale! The fluked tail of
another can be seen beyond the bow of the ship from
which the barrel has been cast. That whale seems
to be following the vessel farthest left. Each of the dozen
ships is in dire peril from savage storm, howling wind,
raging sea, and the unleashed strength of these
leviathans.

Again there are puzzles within puzzles, like a nest
of Chinese boxes. Does this perhaps depict the Biblical
story of Jonah, at the point before the decision to
throw him overboard? Is it an allegory of man pursued
by sin? Does the church tower illuminated on the
horizon suggest salvation and spiritual safety?

The power of this picture does not depend on
accepting any one of such possible answers. This is, first
of all, a panorama of enormous menace and dark
mood. It reveals a disturbed, almost distraught spirit
in the painter—yet what a masterly achievement to
present it by means never before attempted!

Here, perhaps more than anywhere else in his career,
Bruegel broke free from established patterns of
painting. Fury is unleashed. Nature is on a rampage.
Man's vessels and devices are in dire jeopardy. The
monsters of the sea pursue closely. Yet somehow the
feeling persists that these hard-driven vessels will
survive after all. Amidst terror and turmoil man is not
wholly the helpless victim of the storm.

That is the final mood, if not the explicit message, of

112 The Triumph of Time;
engraving by Philip Galle,
dated 1574 (Los Angeles)

TEMPVS OMNIA ET SINGVLA CONSVMENS.

Solis equus, Lunæque, inuectum quattuor Horis,   Proripiunt Tempus curru quod præpete secum   Pone subit, cunctis rebus Fama vna superstes,
Signa per extenti duodena volubilis Anni,   Cuncta rapit comiti Morti non rapta relinquens.   Gætulo boue vecta, implens clangoribus orbem.

this amazing storm-seascape. Without a single symbol
to point directly to events in Bruegel's final years,
it reveals more than perhaps any other one painting how
deeply agitated and torn was his inmost spirit.

One wonders, in the face of a work so somber and
cataclysmic as this, or a study as intense and tragic
as that of *The Parable of the Blind*, how generation after
generation could regard Bruegel as "Droll Peter" or
"Peasant" Bruegel, a laugh-provoker and funnyman of
Flemish art. The reason was partly ignorance, partly a
lack of sensitivity, but also the slavish habit of many
critics repeating with minor variations what others had
said earlier on the same subject.

In several powerful works Bruegel dealt with "last
things" and with the inescapable fact of human
mortality. One of these, an elaborate and sweeping
allegory based on classic myths, is like a strange
commentary by Bruegel on the realizations that come
to many thoughtful men as they see time destroying the
objects of human ambition or power, and finally taking
away life itself. This work is called *The Triumph of
Time*.

His own drawing does not survive. However, in
1574, five years after Bruegel's death, Philip Galle began
publishing prints from an engraving that had been made
from that lost original [112].

As usual, the Latin inscriptions beneath are keyed
closely to the content of the picture. The title in capital
letters at lower center means TIME CONSUMING EACH
AND ALL. The half-dozen lines of Latin verse are reflected
in the pictured action: "The horses of the Sun and
Moon hurry Time forward. Carried by the four Seasons
through the twelve signs of the revolving year [the
signs of the zodiac], he bears off everything with him as
he travels on his rapid chariot, leaving what he has not
seized to Death, his companion. They are followed
by Fame, the last survivor of all things, carried on an
elephant, filling the world with the blasts of her
trumpet."

The savage figure standing on the strange wagon is
Father Time, or Chronos. He is indeed a shocking
father: a cannibal who devours his own offspring.

The cannibalism fits the allegory exactly, however;
for Time, the symbolic parent of all things, also sooner
or later destroys or consumes them all!

Bruegel places the grim Time-Death-Fame procession into a Low Countries background: rural village and countryside at right, the sea and shore at left.

The horses labeled Sun and Moon appear to be plodding rather than galloping. Time's chariot is a wagon. Its wheels symbolize the changing seasons. In front is the leafy foliage of springtime; in back, the barren branches of winter.

The wagon bears a great globe of the earth, with much geographic detail, including a sailing vessel on its oceans. Around that geographic globe are all twelve signs of the Zodiac, as used by astronomers and astrologers for so long. Among others we see the Crab, the Fish, the Lion, the Bull, the Ram, the Twins, and the Scorpion. A great tree grows out of this Earth. In its branches is a sixteenth century "alarm clock," driven by falling weights. Every kind of astronomical and terrestial time-keeping device is suggested here.

Behind Time rides Death, a hooded skeleton bearing a scythe, in the traditional form of the Grim Reaper. Further still behind comes Fame, riding a most morose and thoughtful-looking elephant, while, cheeks puffed, she blows her loud trumpet.

Time himself, while clutching his unfortunate infant son in his right hand, holds aloft in the left a living ring, formed from a snake with its tail in its mouth. This is a familiar symbol of the unending cycle or sequences of events, and especially of life itself.

It is on the roadway, under the feet of the beasts and the wheels of the Time chariot, that Bruegel has placed the most abundant and suggestive assortment of symbols drawn from social living. These are the emblems of human rank, power, attainment, and skill. And all are being crushed or spurned by this remorseless juggernaut: the chariot of Time.

Many levels in human society are indicated: the crown and scepter of the ruler; the cardinal's hat of the ecclesiastic prince; the helmet, sword, and spear of the soldier; the hat of the burgher or merchant; the tools of manual workers and craftsmen; the treasure chest and silver plate of the rich man; and others.

Instruments of the arts, too, lie scattered along this highway, as if in a great symbolic junkyard. There are stringed and wind musical instruments; a book that lies open, as if dropped half-read, a broken column suggesting architecture and building; and still more.

Just ahead of the forefeet of Fame's elephant lie the artist's palette, tufted brush, and the stick for steadying the hand that will no more paint. Bruegel has included just about everything of importance.

The background holds much that is typical of him. Birds fly in the sky. At right, amidst Flemish village buildings, including a church, peasants dance around a kind of Maypole in a square. Nearer, a lad and lass walk together. Amidst the pleasures of the folk festival and the courting couple there seems little awareness of the grim allegory of Time, the terrible cannibal.

Bruegelisms appear also in left background. Just past the face of Death, a small sailboat is seen in the distance. It appears to be in danger as it is driven near shore. Above, and still more distant in the scene, a coastal town is aflame. Great plumes of fire and smoke are swept up into the sky.

The composition as a whole is static. It is loaded, perhaps overloaded, with weighty symbols. Its content makes it peculiarly indicative of the concerns and attitudes of this thoughtful man and artist.

The Fame suggested in this engraving is not necessarily favorable. It is the reputation—good, mediocre, or poor—that arises in the world about the individual no longer alive. This stresses the drastic differences that may arise between what a man was, or believed himself to be, in life, and what the world comes to believe about him after Time and Death triumph.

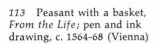

113 Peasant with a basket, *From the Life*; pen and ink drawing, c. 1564-68 (Vienna)

In the case of an artist so superbly able to communicate his view of the world as Bruegel, the distortions of posthumous Fame may be less than for others. There are, after all, his enduring works themselves to correct the brazen trumpetings of Fame, when they sound too far off-key. Though works of art, too, are finally swept into the discard by Time, they may long outlast the life that produced them.

The record of Bruegel's fame or repute since 1569, with all its changes, does seem to confirm the comfort

that Shakespeare offered in the opening lines of his
Sonnet 55:

> Not marble, nor the gilded monuments
> Of princes, shall outlive this powerful rime . . .

For Shakespeare's "rime," substitute Bruegel's art. It
has already outlived many a marble and gilded
monument of princes.

In Bruegel's breathtaking final works he had moved
from multiplicities to subtle simplicities. He had come
closer to recognizable realities, yet never fallen to
the level of flat, merely photographic recording. He
molded the familiar elements around him into patterns
new, expressive, often terrible and tragic, yet never
uncontrolled or trite.

Amidst years of increasingly trying and disruptive
events, he had progressed ever more surely into his final
masteries. His direction was toward greater participation,
greater sympathy and empathy with the lives, the
labors, the fears, hopes, amusements, miseries, and the
resistances of the masses of people around him.

Much of his finest work remains veiled or even
baffling in specific meanings. Its cryptic character
reflects both the outward terrors of the last years of his
working life and the special symbols and insights that
came to form his private world. Yet the power and
beauty and intrinsic interest of even his most puzzling
pictures are never in doubt. One feels the merit of the
thought even when one cannot reduce it to phrases or
statements.

One may justifiably speak of *worlds*, in the plural,
in connection with Bruegel's art. This book has explored
some of those particular worlds. Bruegel was the
faithful recorder of nature and man's labors amidst
nature. He was the fantasist and early surrealist who
raised to a new level the significant and haunting
imaginations of Hieronymus Bosch. He was a master of
the didactic, or teaching, picture, exposing the excesses
and follies of the false world and of the egotistic
individuals shaped by it.

Bruegel was the pictorialist who provided faithful
Flemish settings and equivalents for great dramatic
scenes based on the Scriptures and sacred legends. From
folksayings and popular proverbs he distilled images,
deepening the meanings and broadening the implications

of familiar phrases.

Bruegel was the master-artist of the waters. In superb fashion he interpreted the sea, the streams, the harbors, estuaries, coasts, and ships. He recorded with rare affection and fidelity man's watery environment, at peace and also in stormy frenzy.

He was the artist who first and best found how to capture the essentials of winter's snows, ice, and emotional atmosphere.

He was the maker of the exuberant multipictures, interweaving the varied activities of scores and hundreds of men, women, children in complex yet astoundingly lucid and effective compositions.

He was an artist devoted to his land, its countryside, towns, villages, customs, curiosities, festivals, follies, and frauds. The best of his art says, in effect, "I, the artist, am human, and nothing human is wholly alien to me."

With all this inclusiveness, his art was intensely individual. It was specific to him, and also to his part of the world, and his era. Its very individuality has endowed it with enduring broad interest. One need not be Flemish nor familiar with Flemish customs and traditions to love Bruegel, though such familiarity may come about sooner or later as a result of that affection.

Bruegel, in sum, was so consummately an artist of abundance that his works unfold continually new levels of reward and pleasure to those who learn to know them.

114 Head of a peasant, *From the Life*; pen and ink drawing, c. 1564–68 (Rotterdam)

PETRO BRVEGEL, PICTORI.

Afterword

Bruegel's artistic abundance and variety find analogies in the artistic achievements of his direct descendants. Both his sons became painters and the fathers of painters. Through his younger son, Jan, in particular, one may trace a line of artists worthy of being called a dynasty.

Even to outline briefly the clan descended from Peter the Elder requires naming about two dozen individuals whose dates of birth and death range from the second half of the sixteenth century well into the eighteenth. Most of them were born and worked in Antwerp or Brussels, but during the seventeenth century some were active and even eminent in Italy or Spain.

Teniers and Van Kessel, two names prominent in art, are intertwined with Bruegel's as a result of the marriages of his granddaughters. In each case three successive generations of painters and artists of some standing were thus added to the Bruegel art clan.

The particular talents of Bruegel's artist-descendants cannot be specified here, but a book as large as this or larger could easily be devoted to the achievements of the ten or dozen most able among them. Only the two sons of the master himself are mentioned briefly here.

The reputation of Jan, also known as "Velvet" or "Paradise" Breughel, has fared far better than that of his older brother Peter the Younger, nicknamed "Hell" Breughel. Their numerous surviving works show strange contrasts. Jan is elegant, fluent, precise. A skilled miniaturist, he mastered the best in the methods of his grandmother, Marie Bessemers Coecke, who was one of his teachers. He became a specialist in the decorative painting of tiny but perfect flowers and fruits, but he also did many a competent landscape. It was his

115 Bartholomeus Spranger, *Peter Bruegel the Elder;* engraved by Egidius Sadeler, undated but made after Bruegel's death

116 Domenicus Lampsonius, *Peter Bruegel the Elder;* engraving from Lampsonius' *Pictorum Aliquot Celebrium Germaniae inferioris effigies,* published in 1572 by the widow of Jerome Cock; probably not a portrait from the life

smoothness that earned him the nickname of "Velvet."

Peter the Younger's works, on the other hand, sometimes seem crude, abrupt, or even incomplete. He often copied or adapted pictures by his father. In fact, Van Mander, writing during his lifetime, declared cruelly that Peter did not paint from life but merely "copies and imitates the work of his father."

The nickname "Hell" was based on the frequency of demonic and hellish subjects among his works. A dictionary of painters and engravers published in New York City in 1903 offered an evaluation of father and sons that is typical of art tastes prevalent in the nineteenth and early twentieth centuries: "In art Jan Breughel was as superior to his father as the latter was to his son Pieter [the Younger]."

The fame of Peter the Elder has grown during recent decades, and there is some indication that amends may be made in part also to Peter the Younger. Georges Marlier, an eminent Belgian art historian who has written the most thorough study of Coecke van Aelst, is working now on a study of Peter the Younger, seeking to give a better-rounded view of his place in art history.

IOANNES BREVGEL
ANTVERPIÆ PICTOR FLORVM ET RVRALIVM PROSPECTVV

Jan merits one very special mention. As he matured, he came to look strikingly like the father whom he had scarcely known. Both he and his brother were drawn by the Flemish master portraitist, Anthony Van Dyck [117, 118]. In these portraits Jan shows the same deep-set, rather sad eyes; the lines from the nose down to the sides of the mouth; the nose shape—all reminders of the surviving portraits of Peter the Elder.

The records of the Bruegel clan of artists contain many an interesting anecdote. In 1637 David Teniers II, an able painter and the son of a painter, married Anna Breughel, daughter of Jan and granddaughter of Peter the Elder. Some fourteen years later, in 1651, Anna and David, now increasingly famous and influential, moved from Antwerp to Brussels. There they took up residence in the same house, at 132 Rue Haute, where Peter the Elder and his wife Maeyken had lived nearly a century before, and where both Peter the Younger and Jan had been born.

It is not hard to see why plans have been made for the restoration of this house, so deeply linked to past glories of Flemish art. It may well become as famed and as frequently visited by art lovers as is the fascinating Rembrandt House in Amsterdam, not very many miles to the north.

PETRVS BREVGEL
ANTVERPIÆ PICTOR RVRALIVM ACTIONVM.

117 Anthony Van Dyck, *Jan Breughel*; engraved and etched by Anthony Van Dyck, c. 1621 (New York). The Latin text indicates that Jan resided in Antwerp, and that he painted especially flowers and rural landscapes.

And in the church of Notre Dame de la Chapelle nearby, where Bruegel was wed and where his body is buried, the site of his grave is marked by an ornate and elaborate memorial, including a grandiose painting by Peter Paul Rubens himself [119], depicting Saint Peter.

But the true glory of Peter Bruegel, artist of abundance, resides neither in memorial marbles nor granite nor gilt and glass. It survives rather in the minds and imaginations of living people whose lives are stimulated and heightened by his paradoxes, his humanity, and the seemingly unending riches revealed in the many-sided legacy of his art.

118 Anthony Van Dyck, *Peter Breughel the Younger*; engraved and etched by Anthony Van Dyck, c. 1621 (New York). The Latin text indicates that Peter the Younger also lived in Antwerp and painted rural activities primarily.

119 Peter Paul Rubens, *Jesus Presenting the Keys to Heaven to Saint Peter*. Painting above the tomb of Peter Bruegel the Elder at the Church of Notre Dame de la Chapelle, Brussels

Works in the United States

California	**Los Angeles** County Museum of Art Prints from engravings after works by Bruegel **San Diego** Timken Art Gallery *Parable of the Sower* (painting, signed and dated, 1557) **San Francisco** Achenbach Foundation for Graphic Arts Prints from engravings after works by Bruegel
Washington, D.C.	The National Gallery of Art *Landscape with the Martyrdom of Saint Catherine of Alexandria* (painting, c. 1553–54; attribution in question) *Landscape with the Temptation of Saint Anthony* (painting, c. 1558; attribution in question) Prints from engravings after works by Bruegel Library of Congress Prints from engravings after works by Bruegel
Illinois	Art Institute of Chicago Prints from engravings after works by Bruegel, including *Landscape with Rabbit Hunters*, etching by Bruegel himself
Indiana	**Indianapolis** Clowes Fund Art Collection *Nocturnal Landscape with a Hermit* (painting, c. 1550; attribution in question)

Maine	**Brunswick** Bowdoin College Museum of Fine Arts *View of Waltersspurg* (drawing, c. 1553)
Massachusetts	**Boston** Museum of Fine Arts *Battle Between Carnival and Lent* (painting; unsigned and undated; attribution doubtful) *Towers and Gates of Amsterdam* (drawing, signed and dated, 1562) Prints from engravings after works by Bruegel, including *Landscape with Rabbit Hunters*, etching by Bruegel himself **Cambridge** Fogg Art Museum *Alpine Landscape* (drawing, c. 1556) **Northampton** Smith College Museum of Art *Mountain Landscape with Four Travelers* (drawing, signed and dated 1560)
Michigan	The Detroit Institute of Arts *The Wedding Dance in the Open Air* (painting, dated 1566)
New York City	The Frick Collection *Three Soldiers* (painting, signed and dated, 1568) The Metropolitan Museum of Art *The Harvesters*, or *The Corn Harvest* (painting, signed and dated, 1565) *The Marriage of Mopsus and Nisa* (drawing, c. 1566) Prints from engravings after works by Bruegel, including *Landscape with Rabbit Hunters*, etching by Bruegel himself New York Public Library Prints from engravings after works by Bruegel The Pierpont Morgan Library *The Large Rhine Landscape* (drawing, signed, c. 1553)
Ohio	The Cleveland Museum of Art *Two Peasants in Half-Length* (drawing, c. 1565)
Pennsylvania	Philadelphia Museum of Art Prints from engravings after works by Bruegel (John G. Johnson Collection) *The Unfaithful Shepherd* (painting, c. 1565; attribution in question) *Village Wedding* (painting, c. 1556; attribution in question)

Index

All paintings, drawings, and engravings are by Peter Bruegel the Elder unless otherwise noted. Pages on which illustrations appear are preceded by an asterisk.